"Radically honest, deeply personal, and comforting. I wanted this book to continue on forever. Natalie puts into words what so many of us have felt over the past four years since the planet was ravaged by a global pandemic, to which not even creativity was immune. And yet, this book is filled with hope. Through her eyes and the tenderness of memory and time, a path back home to the heart of what matters is illuminated, both for herself, and for all of us."

—**Aomawa Shields, PhD**, astrophysicist and author of *Life on Other Planets*

"*Writing on Empty* is far from being another book about writer's block. Zen wisdom teaches that underneath being is not being. Likewise, the underbelly of knowing is not knowing—and perhaps the backbone of writing is not writing. . . . Here as she travels the terrain of loss and longing, we experience Natalie at her most tender and exquisite." —**Ann Filemyr, PhD**, poet and president, Southwestern College, Santa Fe, NM

"*Writing on Empty* is part memoir, part writing manual, and a full meditation on emptiness. . . . A touching and powerful book detailing her struggle to find meaning and motivation during a desperate time. Even on empty, Goldberg's prose is at its finest as she shares her emotional and geographic terrain with the clarity, wisdom, heart, and humor we expect from this beloved writer."

—**Steve Reigns**, author of *A Quilt for David*

"The naked truth about writing! It doesn't always flow but it never fails to connect us with life—our own life and the life of the world. With fierce honesty, feisty humor, and relentless determination, one of the greatest teachers of our times uses her own process to show us the way to be so present in the fallow seasons that we cannot help but break through to a more vibrant intimacy with things as they are, and a renewed capacity for sharing them."

—**Mirabai Starr**, author of *Wild Mercy*
and *Caravan of No Despair*

"In this remarkable book, Natalie Goldberg's rich and wild mind brings us to the landscape of emptiness and then delivers us from sorrow. This fascinating book is full of pathos, humor, gorgeous detail, then beauty and surprise. It is a powerful revelation about this very moment and about the truth of our lives that is often hidden from us. One learns and leaps, and falls back and moves forward on this path of discovery unfolded by this marvelous writer."

—**Rev. Joan Jiko Halifax**, Abbot, Upaya Zen Center

WRITING ON EMPTY

ALSO BY NATALIE GOLDBERG

Three Simple Lines: A Writer's Pilgrimage into the Heart and Homeland of Haiku

Let the Whole Thundering World Come Home: A Memoir

The Great Spring: Writing, Zen, and This Zigzag Life

Living Color: Painting, Writing, and the Bones of Seeing

The True Secret of Writing: Connecting Life with Language

Old Friend from Far Away: The Practice of Writing Memoir

The Great Failure: My Unexpected Path to Truth

Top of My Lungs: Poems and Paintings

Thunder and Lightning: Cracking Open the Writer's Craft

The Essential Writer's Notebook

Banana Rose: A Novel

Long Quiet Highway: Waking Up in America

Wild Mind: Living the Writer's Life

Writing Down the Bones: Freeing the Writer Within

Chicken and in Love: Poems

WRITING ON EMPTY

A Guide to
FINDING YOUR VOICE

NATALIE GOLDBERG

ST. MARTIN'S
ESSENTIALS
NEW YORK

First published in the United States by St. Martin's Essentials,
an imprint of St. Martin's Publishing Group

WRITING ON EMPTY. Copyright © 2024 by Natalie Goldberg.
All rights reserved. Printed in the United States of America.
For information, address St. Martin's Publishing Group,
120 Broadway, New York, NY 10271.

www.stmartins.com

Designed by Steven Seighman

The Library of Congress Cataloging-in-Publication Data
is available upon request.

ISBN 978-1-250-34254-6 (hardcover)
ISBN 978-1-250-34255-3 (ebook)

Our books may be purchased in bulk for promotional, educational,
or business use. Please contact your local bookseller or the Macmillan
Corporate and Premium Sales Department at 1-800-221-7945, extension
5442, or by email at MacmillanSpecialMarkets@macmillan.com.

First Edition: 2024

10 9 8 7 6 5 4 3 2 1

For Jacqueline West

a Thousand Thank-yous

CONTENTS

Rose

A ripe pear cannot be young again

A horse has just so many years to live

Do not say anything

Let the past go

I reach my hand back through the leaves

no skull   no mouth

I left you in a yellow book

I left you on the backyard table

Why hold on any more?

Where is that silver pearl?

no beach to swim

no sand   no luncheon counter

Still there is a taste of honey

And don't those petals forgive

Everything as they fall?

—N.G.

INTRODUCTION

ALL THE POETS and writers, painters, and musicians I knew stopped dead during Covid. None of us could create. For me, no café, library, or coffee shop—where I often write—was open. Many of the beautiful parks of my beloved New Mexico—its landscape my wellspring—were also closed. I froze.

I was miserable and vacant. I needed to separate from the house, the dishes, the phone calls, in order to begin writing again. I was lost with no way home.

Out of desperation, I decided to return to Port Townsend, a place where I had had two writing residencies. It was a place where I was happy. I rented a small apartment there to try to find myself again.

On March 16, 2022, I flew in to spend my first night in the new rental. I woke at 3 A.M., disoriented, went into the bathroom in the dark, and fell face-first into the iron tub, my legs in the air. I hit my nose and forehead, hard. Stunned, I wasn't sure I could get up. I pushed with both hands, found my feet on the ground, returned to bed, and sat upright, leaning against the wall, waiting for daylight.

When first light came through the window, I ignored my throbbing head, grabbed my laptop, which was on the other end of the bed, and joined a writing group that a student of mine was conducting on Zoom. I'd never joined her group before and I wrote two writing exercises with them. The writing was innocuous, but I wanted to write. To connect. (I didn't write about what had just happened.) After the Zoom session, I closed the computer and said: "Okay, I'm ready to drive to Urgent Care." I made my way there slowly in the rented car, not daring to look at myself in the rearview mirror.

The nurse took one look at me, ordered a wheelchair, and rolled me to the emergency section of the hospital across the way. After receiving an MRI and X-rays three hours later, the doctor on call pronounced: "Nothing broken and no blood in your brain," and wrote a prescription for physical therapy.

Driving home, I passed the food co-op. *My fridge is empty,* I thought, and turned into the parking lot. I wore a mask, thinking no one could see me. No one would recognize me. But as I headed back to my car, groceries in hand, I passed a woman I knew slightly from two years before. She stopped short, her eyes wide, and exclaimed, "What happened to you? Your nose is twice the size."

"I fell," I responded, embarrassed. She kindly said she would visit later in the day. Really, I knew no one else there. Usually I long for solitude, but in this situation, I needed people.

In a daze I pulled out of the parking lot and backed into another car. The owner got out and banged on my window. I rolled it down, and she said, "Didn't you see me? I kept honking my horn."

I shook my head, no.

"Well, you didn't hurt my car. I don't know about yours." She got back into her car and drove off.

I, too, drove off, not daring to look at my car's rear end.

After five continuous days of resting on the couch in a daze, paging through piles of *New Yorker*s and part of a novel, I finally said, "Nat, you're a Zen person. Just sit here, for heaven's sake." I put down all distractions.

That lasted twelve minutes. I opened my eyes and turned my head. A stack of old spiral notebooks was on the coffee table. I had been writing but had no inspiration. I reached for one, opened it, and read. Halfway through the first notebook, I looked up: "Shit, this is really good. You have to write a book about this empty time!" (I often talk to myself.)

So I did, and here it is: how I faced the void, survived, and eventually found my way out.

PART I

THE WRITER'S PANDEMIC

We really really really don't have much time left.
—Grove

THE END OF June. The virus is raging. Nothing is open. No place I can escape to write except the great outdoors, where I go and find a bench in a secret alcove. The park is not far from my house. It's a dry place where I live; I bring water and it's private enough, but there are so many people with their dogs—everyone seems to have canines but me. We all stay distant from one another.

The pandemic officially started for me on March 12, a Thursday. I was supposed to be in conversation with Jenn Shapland, the author of *My Autobiography of Carson Mc-Cullers,* at a downtown bookstore, but an hour before the scheduled time, both Jenn and I canceled. The bookstore owner was furious. Anyone who showed up had to turn around and go home. We promised that in two months—

when the scare was over—to reconvene and fulfill our commitment.

It wouldn't last, this scare. Wasn't this the good old USA? We would pull through. Think of World War II. Did we not save the world?

I had been looking forward to discussing that book, which was nominated for a National Book Award, about Carson McCullers. I had loved Carson since ninth grade and found out only recently, because there was so much hidden about women in the Fifties and Sixties, that in the last years of her life she was in a relationship with a woman. She was happy, which made me happy. McCullers had suffered so much—she had her first stroke in her twenties; she died at fifty.

The art museum in Columbus, Georgia, finally had an exhibit about the hometown girl on her centennial year, in the basement. I traveled to see it. There was a photo of Carson heartily grinning in the back seat of a convertible with her honey, who was driving. It was clear they were in a relationship. Shapland addressed Carson's lesbianism in her new book, and I was glad.

In mid-March no one was wearing masks, which made Jenn and me even more nervous about convening the interview publicly.

Two months later, I watched over and over on all kinds of media the immovable knee on the back of George Floyd's neck in front of witnesses. Floyd was murdered on the asphalt street near where I taught reading in the early Eighties in a Minneapolis public school.

I still think of my student Philip, his skinny ninth-grade legs. His two brothers, a junior and senior, would stop by the class. Philip wore a too-large olive-green crew-neck sweater against the murderous cold of Minnesota. "Ms. Goldberg, are you black? You're not white. And you don't shave your legs." He came to this conclusion in spring when I wore a skirt and Birkenstocks.

"You sure are patient," he said. "How can you wait for me to figure out words?"

"Philip, when you relax, you can read perfectly well."

That was the key. These kids were told they couldn't read; they were marked.

I think of cheerful Anita, who told me she watched TV at home. One morning she came in and eyed me closely. "Last night on this show they were talking about medi-tation." She imitated crossed legs, closed eyes, hands on knees. "You look like one of 'em."

I jumped up on a desktop and showed her the position.

"Goldberg, you're too much," she said.

I've often wondered if my students are still alive. It was my favorite job ever.

It was dawning on me that this pandemic was going to go on a long time.

My grandfather immigrated to the United States in the late 1800s. Every day, he sat in his folding lawn chair in the driveway in front of the garage door of our split-level off Hempstead Turnpike, wearing his brown suit, fedora hat, reading the Yiddish paper with an unlit stogie on his lower lip. He greeted me after school each day. "Darling, you just don't know how good we have it. There is nothing like America." My grandparents were filled with so much hope. My grandfather had escaped the draft in Russia, which hated Jews. The army would have taken him for his whole life. As a child his wife, Rosie, ran from the pogroms in Poland. At the turn of the twentieth century, the US let in immigrants fairly freely. I loved my grandparents and believed my grandfather with all my heart, ingested my grandpa's vision, the huge beautiful America, this narrative of the Land of the Free. It was that way for him. And something in me wanted to believe it, too, though even as a young child, I could see the terrible injustice that Black people faced in the US, and it disturbed me.

For centuries in many European countries, Jews were forced to live in ghettos, not allowed to budge. What's it like out there where we could not go, where the Christians settled? This must have rung in my mind, like the Liberty Bell. I made a close friend with a poet from Nebraska. Did they have Jews out there? What does a girl from Brooklyn know? In my imagination Nebraska contained emptiness, a commodity I longed for after centuries of crowded shtetls. This past life was all communicated unconsciously. I was born here, but I still thought: *Jew gets to have a friend in small-town America.* I kept saying this to myself. For a time, I even had a boyfriend. I rode on the back of his motorcycle through summer rainstorms to an afternoon movie theater. We parked on a corner of broken sidewalks with patches of grass interspersed with patches of mud. Worms gathered on the little cement that was left. The theater was mostly empty, with velvet seats, and we gripped large bags of popcorn.

This was the life I read about in Larry McMurtry's *The Last Picture Show.* A slow, small town, this time in Texas, characters with no ambition, no success, just living their lives, a young boy, mentally disabled, sweeping the street. Loneliness abounds, a high school senior has an affair with the desperate wife of the football coach; the owner of the pool hall is in love with the rich man's wife and she's in love with him but neither attempts to change. The one big change is death. It was exotic. I wanted all this, the place where nothing seemed to happen, but you belonged there. You didn't move on.

Through our mutual admiration of Larry McMurtry, I met Eddie Lewis at a writers' conference back when we were both young. I never thought to ask him why he loved McMurtry. But he did. And through that, we had a natural connection.

The friendship bobbled along. He married Mary and they lived on the outskirts of Santa Fe; I moved to Taos for twenty years. We stayed in touch, went to a writing workshop together on the Oregon coast; for seven years we ran a book club that assigned books by African writers. His two sons grew up and moved away.

When Covid hit we found ourselves living at opposite ends of Santa Fe. The time dragged. I stayed close to home. In early May, I spoke to Eddie on the phone: "I go to this park near my house—foot of Canyon Road— called Water History Park. Big trees and shade and green grass." Those attributes are a big commodity in the dry Southwest.

Eddie suggested we meet there the next Wednesday. I had two folding chairs in the car trunk. We unloaded the chairs and water bottles and dragged them to sit near a fence under shade. We sat six feet away, masks on.

Twenty minutes in, Eddie said, "I'll take mine off, if you do."

I looked around. No park police. Neither of us wanted Covid. His forty-year-old son had got it in Dallas at the very beginning and it was hell.

"I'll get a chair of my own," he said as we folded them to return to my car. I could see his mind calculating. "Let's meet here every week for two hours."

"Okay," I said. It was an attempt to find solace.

After we settled the next time, Eddie suggested, "Let's tell each other about our childhoods."

"Okay, tell me again why you never liked your mother," I asked, jumping in. I never quite remembered it right. He was sent away in ninth grade to a Massachusetts boarding school.

"I didn't trust her. She removed us from our house." His brothers had been in the same boarding school in different grades. "All that time my brothers and I never talked to each other. Like we were strangers."

"How come you never talked?" I asked. It seemed odd.

Eddie paused, thinking this over. "First, adolescents are somewhat tribal by nature; that group is more important than family. But also, boys in high school don't sit around talking like you and I do. It's all magnified in boarding school—everything's structured: sports, study hall, meals. To actually break loose and see your brother would require something like making a date.

"But mostly in our family, we were always on our own. That's the basic message of boarding school: you have no family; it's up to you."

Deep in the Covid months, the world around us was painfully changing, and this was our escape. Under the tall trees, the sun in New Mexico strong, we talked of a past life.

"What friends did you have?" Eddie asked me.

"I only had two friends. Denise Hodges. Moon-faced, she wore a little makeup, even in junior high. Her mother wore spiked heels, red lipstick, made hamburgers in a frying pan on top of the stove, while she cracked gum. I guess she was pretty."

"Who?" he asked.

"The mother, but Denise, too. She always had boyfriends, never went to college. I think she married early

11

and got a job out Conklin Avenue—or was it called 110? Where my father had the Aero Tavern. Denise never left the area. I just liked her." I forgot to mention that we spent a whole weekend practicing to try out for cheerleading, repeating the movements: F-I-T-E, F-I-T-E. Flick of the wrist, hop on one foot, yelling loud. Neither of us got in. I don't remember caring.

"And then there was Phyllis Di Giovanni. Feels like a lifetime ago," I said when Eddie and I met and began recounting our memories the next week. "Her father drove a garbage truck. They were Italian. Maybe Denise was French. We all were immigrant families, mostly Irish and Italian Catholic. Not a lot of Jews. Christmas in our split-level development, the houses were all lit up." I show by opening and closing my palms. "Lights, lights, lights, blank, lights, lights. We were the blanks. We had a menorah in the window in early December for Chanukah.

"Just recently Phyllis's fifty-year-old daughter called me. Phyllis died in 2011, a long time ago. We lost touch when I went away to college. She accelerated and did high school in three years, drove each day out to Queen's College. At least an hour away. She drove a sturdy basic white car with a clutch at the steering wheel. I went one day with her and sat in on all her classes. The sociology class was so big, at least 350 students in a lecture hall. Phyllis took notes as I stared at everyone. The professor was talking about something—can't quite remember what—but it was so obvious. I told her when it let out, 'They have a whole course on that?' She grimaced. We were standing in the doorway and everyone was bumping us as they left.

"We went outside, sat on a bench, and ate the lunch her mother packed for us. Egg salad sandwiches. I loved being with Phyllis, but the surroundings were so dull. Small efforts to plant trees surrounded by cement. Next we went to a philosophy class and the teacher in front droned on about Immanuel Kant. I whispered to her, 'I can't, I Kant!' She giggled behind her hand, but she was ever dutiful, taking notes. I wanted to rip the notebook out of her hands, but I also understood. She wanted to make good. I wanted to stand up in the class and say, *Do you realize who you have here? She will be famous some-day. She is remarkable already.* Everyone leaning over their books, it was a commuter college in Queens. Probably full of children of immigrants, but I didn't understand that then. At the end of the day, walking through the parking lot back to the car, 'I wish you could come every day,' she told me. 'I feel so lonely here.'

"She'd study nights at her parents' dining room table after she drove home.

"They lived in the Cape Cods opposite our split-level development on the other side of Hempstead Turnpike. A Cadillac dealer moved in on the corner. Next to it was Zorn's Poultry. We'd get out of the car and look at the peacocks and capons in cages. Phyllis was only a mile away but we couldn't cross the Turnpike. Denise lived four blocks away in the same development as Phyllis.

The housing was all new, with spindly trees planted at the curb, and in the woods in the back of our house they built a factory. Instead of complaining, my parents called it 'progress.' It was the Fifties and early Sixties."

Eddie kept nodding. He was listening closely.

"My uncle Sam, my father's older brother, died somewhere during that time and he didn't mention my father in the will. My father worked behind the bar, drying glasses, thinking throughout every afternoon at work, *All that love wasted*. He didn't care about getting anything, he just wanted a last word from his brother."

"And Phyllis?"

"Oh, yeah, at the end of her sophomore year she met a friend of her brother Ernie. I think he was from New Jersey and his family was rich. Nursing homes and then maybe hotels.

"Eddie, she was real smart," I said as I leaned in. "In sixth grade in front of the whole assembly she was awarded the best all-around student. It was a big public school. Her father was in the audience, put two fingers in his mouth and whistled loud, real loud. I looked over. There he was in his gray work shirt.

"She and I had an intense relationship—not about boys—ideas, books, we were searching. She was my friend all through public school. I guess when she hooked up with this guy I was disappointed, like she copped out, never finished college, but who could blame her? Things all probably felt dead end for her, but in my heart, I blamed her. She was my support for something different, not weird, just an alternative to marriage and children.

"Years later, when I lived in New Mexico, had a few books out, she reached out to me. Always vague and when I called back, she was never available. I didn't get it." The shadows were moving. I was in the sun, moved my chair. "Her daughter told me she had been fighting cancer for years—she never mentioned that to me. Also, she said it was a tumultuous marriage. A waiter in Taos used to work for Phyllis on the east coast and he somehow knew we'd been friends. One day when he was placing a salad in front of me, he said the husband went out with someone from the office and everyone knew.

"Even then he said, 'She had such dignity.'

"Yeah, that was Phyllis. She had great posture, a straight spine. I loved her, Eddie. When her daughter called last week it all came together. I felt bad that I rejected her when she met her husband, but we went in two different directions, and I wasn't that conscious. But now I'm missing her, feel it deep down, want her to be alive so we could talk again. Her daughter told me she was always reading and in the family business she had three thousand employees under her. Her original family were immigrants. They did the best they could. Her brother Ernie joined the business. She sacrificed herself for the family. Her daughter Meredith— nice name, Meredith—says Phyllis was frustrated, always wanted to go back and complete college."

Eddie had to move into the shade.

Hardly anyone came to the park midafternoon in the early months of Covid. At around four o'clock they'd convene with their dogs.

"Once I stayed over at her house and we each drank a whole beer in the basement—I'd never drunk alcohol before. We were sixteen. I vomited the whole night. The next morning, her parents, instead of being mad, were amused I couldn't hold it down.

"Meredith told me that Ernie, Phyllis's brother, was dead, too. Not cancer, something else at seventy-four. So, the whole family I knew is dead. Phyllis died so young. Sixty-one—and fought so long before that."

Just then a long cloud in the shape of a train floated by. I pointed but Eddie couldn't see it, the sun in his eyes. Plus, I had a feeling he was thinking.

"You both wanted to break out. But even though you came from the same place, you took different paths. She sacrificed herself for her family. She didn't have the support probably to break the traditional mode of wife and children. She tried, but the idea of family sucked her back."

Now I was quiet. "Eddie, you're missing one thing. She was first generation. They don't get away, at least women don't seem to. She had to save them, protect them."

Eddie leaned on his elbows. "Yeah, but from what you've told me, in your family, you weren't even on the radar. Remember when you came back from a tennis match in high school, third singles, and your family was eating dinner and didn't even notice you were missing?"

I smiled at that. "You remember? I'm flattered. My old girlfriend thought I was lucky. She said, 'Such freedom,' but it had its own pain and a lot of loneliness."

Eddie was right there with me. "Nat, you were like a person on a space walk; the tether to the mothership came loose. You were utterly off the map, on your own from the day you were born." I held up a part of the moth-eaten sweater I was wearing.

"Eddie, again, I am second generation. My grandparents almost never left Brooklyn until they came out to the suburbs to be with my mother. And before that, she and my father lived with them.

"Maybe second generation gave me the freedom to wander. I could go out and see America—all that praise my grandfather gave it, but he never dreamed of going beyond where he landed after Ellis Island. Also, I don't think he was thinking about land: he meant freedom to be a Jew and be left alone. I took it further. Freedom to travel, to see the whole place—I've been to every state but Alabama. Come to think of it, my father, after the war, was going to spend a year driving around the country. He was first generation, like Phyllis. He got as far as Saratoga Springs, discovered gambling, and blew all of his money on horses at the racetrack." I threw up my arms. "He came back to his family broke, had to find a job, and met my mother."

The next week was Eddie's turn. We had shared a lot over the years, but sitting across from each other under the dry air of New Mexico in terrible 2020, the layers built. Who else cared? We cared: it was a Monday.

"It was a football game, an away game—not at Brooks, some anonymous New England prep campus, green grass as far as you can see, trees lining roads, fall colors dotting the woods. Running up and down the field, tackling, being tackled."

"So you were on the wrestling and the football team?"

He nodded, but he was far away—on the East Coast, over fifty years ago. "I looked over at the sidelines and there he was, a long city overcoat and one of those hats men used to wear, black rimmed, glasses. No time to look twice, but I'm sure it was him. My father. Later, after the game, though, he was nowhere to be found, as if he had to get back to the city for an appointment."

"You sure it was him?" When I was young, I didn't know prep schools existed.

"Positive," he said, nodding his head up and down.

"What about before that, before you had to go away?"

"It was the end of childhood. Ninth grade was when each of us was sent away. I couldn't believe it. The walls of our dorm rooms didn't go up to the ceiling, and at night I'd hear someone crying—homesick—and someone else jerking off. Before that, at home I did terrible in school and didn't care. My mother would yell at me, 'You could do better,' but it didn't faze me. I was happy riding my bike all over the neighborhood till dark."

"You must have done well at Brooks to get into Harvard?"

"Yeah, if you didn't do your homework at Brooks, you'd have to stay in study hall and do it there. I wasn't going to be locked in that room. It was bad enough."

All week I'd think about what Eddie and I had talked about. Forever that faraway image of his father. (My father was right at the dinner table at five before the night shift, my mother and grandmother serving him T-bone steak, a wedge of iceberg lettuce, and two quarters of a pale tomato. Often, we ate later, after he left.)

Our favorite topic was talking about a book we had both read: *Short Nights of the Shadow Catcher,* about Edward Curtis, the photographer who, starting in 1900, spent more than three decades taking over forty thousand images of Native Americans and their culture. Eddie's father had bought some Edward Curtis photos and left them to his sons.

"Your father collected art?" I said. "I wish I could have met him." We also admired *Heavy* by memoirist Kiese Laymon and Robert Caro's biographies of Lyndon Johnson.

The next week we turned to how I was going to get into senior housing. My friend Helen was eighty-eight and ecstatic in a residency in California's Portola Valley near hiking trails and nature. I still hiked and seemed in good shape, but I knew where I was heading. I also knew they gave a test when you apply. Helen told me about it. They name five objects at the beginning, and at the end of the twenty-minute interview you had to remember the five words. Helen had a friend who wasn't sharp enough, got rejected. I was still very here, but what was the name of that town, that mountain, that author? I could tell you all about the author's life, but, dammit, the name, the word?

The memories of those afternoons are still fresh in my mind. I remember it like this: settled into our lawn chairs, it is cold this one afternoon, but the sun is strong. The sun had shifted many times over these last few months, but we are in the same park, near the same pine. Sometimes the shadow is too cold. We get in the sun. Then the sun is too hot; we move back to shadow.

"Okay, who goes first?" Both of us start laughing. We are testing memory—getting me ready for Portola Valley, that future answer to aging.

"I'll go," I say.

Eddie jots down five concrete, non-associative words. You can't use *bathing suit,* next to *pool,* next to *water.* The connection helps too much. The stark, unconnected objects must hold forth in hard reality by themselves.

"You ready?"

I sit up straight, alert, like a dog waiting for a bone.

"Record, cloud, millet—"

"Wait a minute. You know *millet?*"—I'm thinking of the hippie years when we baked millet breads following directions in *The Tassajara Bread Book.* Eddie was never a hippie, never took acid or, for that matter, smoked marijuana—"Where did you get *millet*?"

"You don't know how to play a violin, but you might give that word to me." We both dissolve into laughter.

"I'll begin again. Now, listen: *record, cloud, millet, neuron, baby.*" He repeats them slowly, then again.

I nod my head, trying to take them in. Already they feel like they slide off a ski slope. I'm afraid to budge. I fold my hands on my lap. Twenty minutes must pass before I can recite them.

"Start talking," he says.

"No, I have to remember my words."

"We have to talk," he says.

"You start," I say, stiff as a board, trying to hold on to the words.

He tells me about Mary, his wife, who read a book about memory. "In Sophocles's time everyone had a memory. That's how they carried their history."

I drift off for a minute and think of Sophocles. "He wrote Oedipus, didn't he? He killed his father and slept with his mother. And I think I have problems? But what a genius Sophocles was. Move over, Freud. I guess Freud learned from those Greeks."

Then I tell him about the Orthodox rabbis who can't bring paper and pen to Yeshiva. They have to walk out of class knowing every word the rabbi said.

"Okay, Nat, what are the words?"

"How should I know?" We both dissolve in laughter

again, but it gets painful. I recite slowly: *record, cloud, millet,* a pause, then *neuron,* a big smile, but I can't remember the last word. "What is it? C'mon."

He shakes his head, finally gives in: *"Baby."*

"What a dumb word," I sneer.

We do two rounds. Eddie's memory is pretty good. He stumbles a bit. The second round for me: *myrtle, peacock, rain, building, massage.*

I tear off the small paper piece where my initial words are and take it home, look at them while I make dinner. I recite them in bed, jump up out of bed to get the list and check again if I got it right.

When I talk to Eddie on the phone three days later, he can still stumblingly recite his words: *window, cat, hemorrhoid, falcon, stove.* All that rigmarole about the Ivy League. Maybe it is true? And my lower-middle-class upbringing? My immigrant grandmother clutching her housecoat with her right hand, her left holding out a glass of freshly squeezed orange juice in the late November New York cold, coming at me as I wait outside with two others for the bus to take me to fourth grade. I turn toward the curb pretending I didn't see her, hoping the bus would come quickly.

Maybe I should have drunk that fresh orange juice?

I confess two weeks later, after we settle into our seats, "I hardly ever slept since my divorce at thirty-two. That's about forty years. I've never told anyone before. Maybe that's why I can't remember words?"

"What?" Eddie's alert.

"The shock of the breakup, I think, cracked open some deep crevice in my psyche—I was too young to understand. I met a Vietnam vet who never slept. He told people, please don't give me your remedies. I feel the same way. His sleeplessness seems obvious. Mine doesn't. I went through war in another lifetime."

I pause. "I can't face no-sleep now, and for the last year I've taken a chip of a benzo every night. I don't care at this stage if I get addicted. Who was it? Some rock star. I remember hearing he died when his doctor illegally gave him a shot for sleep. I sympathize. You can get really desperate. Sleep leaves your body and you are marooned.

"My partner Yu-kwan sleeps so well I could hang her upside down in a meat locker and she'd have a full night. Sometimes I lie really close and try to imitate her breath. It doesn't help. She tells me, 'Just listen to the clock ticking. It will put you to sleep.'

"I tell her, 'You have to be kidding.'

"Sleep is not natural to me anymore. Robert Johnson is said to have sold his soul to the devil to play the guitar that well." I throw up my hands. "I want to meet that devil: gimme sleep, I'll do whatever you want."

Then we move on to the next subject. I ask Eddie how he began to write.

"I had this English teacher, Graham. I was in ninth grade. He was my wrestling coach, my English teacher, and also became my mentor. He magically opened the door on writing for me." Eddie bends closer. "I can remember the exact moment." I nod my head, listening closely. "It was the first writing assignment of the first class. The assignment had to be done that night, to write directions to our house, where we lived. Our home. Like most of the other students, I was baffled, even incredulous. We were boarders and thought that maybe he didn't fully understand: our homes were hundreds of miles away. We thought hundreds of miles might mean hundreds of pages. Graham was unimpressed." Eddie smiles. "'You know how to get there, don't you?' was all he said.

"That night as I labored over my notebook, something happened. Some force of gravity lifted. Explanation changed to instinct. Like a complex wrestling maneuver you've learned and practiced over and over, but you assume you would never use, and then suddenly there you are in the finals of the New England Championships unleashing that move on your opponent as if you own it.

"All the possibilities of writing opened up for me—I scribbled directions to the Eastern Airlines ticket counter at Logan Airport, then once in Washington, how to find a taxi. I felt the narrative power of taking a reader from point A to point B, the responsibility of being exact with language; a wrong left turn and you were lost. And most strongly, for the first time I felt my life, my house, could legitimately be the subject of what I wrote." Eddie takes a big gulp of air. He is really in it. "I never got over the promise of writing."

We are both silent for a moment. I can hear the leaves above our heads fluttering.

And then, "Sooo?" He opens his palms. "What about you?"

"Do we have time?" I ask.

"If you're not too long-winded." We both burst out laughing.

"I was mad for literature. You know, even in the *public schools*"—I lift my right eyebrow for emphasis—"I had two great English teachers. Mr. Cates lived near us in a ranch house. This was what he was like: each summer he chose an author and read everything they wrote. He made us think; he was demanding. Even now, with every book I write, I pause at some point and think, would Mr. Cates approve? He died in 1987, quit teaching a year or two before and moved down to Key West where his sister lived. He was sixty-two." I choke up. "How can I ever repay Mr. Cates? It is so long ago and the books still ring in me: *The Brothers Karamazov, The Ballad of the Sad Café.*"

Eddie, leaning forward, is listening intensely.

"Shit," I say and wipe the tears with my sleeve.

"Mr. Clemente, too, but I've talked about him so many other times."

It's time to go.

We fold our chairs, throw them in the trunks. I stand behind my car, watch the tick-tick-tick of his right directional. Then a left onto Camino Cabre. This day I'm slow to leave the park.

That night I go home and ask my partner about *her* boarding school experience. It was the opposite of Eddie's. She was starving in Hong Kong when her mother married an English army corporal who was stationed there after World War II. They sent her to a British boarding school. Until then, she hadn't known that people ate three meals a day. She always remembers the food. "They were constantly feeding us. Breakfast was three courses: eggs and bacon, fruits and cereal, hot oatmeal." She takes a deep breath. "At ten thirty we had a break for hot cocoa and buns. Lunchtime was a three-course affair, and at five thirty, kippers or scones and tea. Some students skipped this. I never did. And dinner at seven was three courses. I never wasted anything on my plate. I went there skinny and gained fifteen pounds." She pauses. "But I didn't speak English. That was hard. I was ten, had no training or discipline before. Everything was regulated; I had to join a language circle, a discussion group. Eventually, I grew to like it because I was learning. It took a while, but no matter what, I never fit in. I was Chinese."

On the following Sunday in the late afternoon, Mary calls. "Eddie had an accident. He is in the hospital."

I hold my breath.

"He crashed on his bike. Luckily, I was right behind him. I ran in the middle of the street where he landed and stopped traffic. He broke his collarbone, six or seven ribs, and his left leg below the knee. He has to be operated on tomorrow, right away. Otherwise, he can't stand."

"Oh." It's all I can say.

"He has to be in a wheelchair for three months."

A long time. "How is he?"

"Mostly he keeps repeating, 'I can't believe I was so stupid.' His wheel got caught and he went flying."

I can tell she is exhausted. We hang up.

In three weeks the three of us were planning to dare the pandemic and drive to Minnesota. Mary is a state native; she'd visit her brothers. I had friends from years ago. I am scared for Eddie. Will he be okay in the end?

At home with no scheduled interruption, I sink into the prospect of no escape. No café, restaurant, museum, bookstore, or library open. Even the Zen Center down the road closed. I tell myself, *It's okay. Take a rest. You've done enough. What else did I want to do? All travel was banned.* The virus gets worse, spreads. I no longer see friends. I wonder if I *have* friends. I have never been home so much. I have a house, food. There's a toilet paper shortage. People are dying, whole families wiped out. My ancient genes kick in. We never went anyplace. I was marooned in the suburbs, back on Long Island in a green split-level. I'm dissolved in claustrophobia.

Hiking becomes too much effort. Picking up a pen and writing is impossible. Why bother? And what would

I write about? I have nothing to say. Why paint? Why do yoga? No book can command my attention. Sitting in a beige plastic chair in the backyard, I surrender to disappointment, bewilderment, inertia. Why do anything?

I lose my appetite. Half a banana? No desire. Finally, the Covid mind has grabbed me. Everything canceled. I'd fought against it. Now I sink deeper and deeper into a dark grief. Other horrors begin to enter with no defense. Old friends dead. Cancer, too, is rampant. The virus almost wipes out the entire Navajo Nation in New Mexico and Arizona. The country is exploding.

I never before had used the word *evil,* explaining it only as a person's solidification of anger or fear, aggression. Solid, but always with the possibility of change. But now, as I read the newspaper, listening to news, it feels that collective forces are pouring through people, no individual choice, more like a cult.

On the phone, long distance, "Nataleee, please explain: What is wrong? People wear masks?" A question from a Japanese colleague.

I try to explain. "Different here. No one ever wore masks. Yes, in Japan it's accepted. Here, they think, not free. I know, makes no sense."

This is the first time I don't have a next book in mind. I never realized what a gift it was: like racehorses waiting in the docket, ready to go, nostrils flared, flanks in poised determination. Book after book, nothing else. Single-minded. At the time it felt like compulsion—as I wrote one, I ached to write the next. I never thought how lucky I was.

I had complained to Eddie one day at the park.

"Well, Natalie, welcome. Now you know how other writers feel."

Slouched in the plastic chair on the back portal, I feel that none of my past writing history mattered. No one cares about books. I bludgeon myself: no one reads. They walk around attached to mechanical contraptions. Besides, Black, Asian, immigrant, refugee voices are finally being heard. *Get out of the way.* The newspapers feature fresh blood, new writers, first books. *Get out of the way.*

I continue: you are the only person left who is still rummaging around old drugstores, searching for cheap spiral notebooks, at $1.56, the old price forty years ago and a color cover you never used before. And all of your pens—they leak. (I still handwrite everything.) You got blue ink all over your fancy yellow bedsheets.

I feel void, shallow, miserable, a nobody. It springs to mind that I am like a Fifties housewife, a pimple on her chin devastating, ruining her day, that insubstantial. I'd read *The Feminine Mystique*. I knew all about those housewives. I'd even been to Betty Friedan's grave out on the tip of Long Island, although it hadn't been a destination; I was visiting the studio of Jackson Pollock. The tour guide knew him and did not have one nice thing to say about him. "A drunk" was pretty much all he indicated. I asked, "What about his groundbreaking drip paintings?"

"So what?" he said. I smiled, having a sense the whole small town felt this way. The guide was disgusted that Pollock received so much postmortem attention. At the end of his talk, he gave a nod with his chin in the direction of a cemetery down the road where we could find his grave.

It was a beautiful place. You wouldn't mind being buried there yourself. Green grass and green deciduous trees. Plenty of space between memorial stones, not lined up in any order. I perused other sites: here was buried Betty Friedan. I never forgot what she wrote: If a housewife has all day to mop the kitchen floor, by the end of the day, she doesn't get to it. If that same woman gets a job, she manages before leaving at eight for work to do all her chores.

Structure liberates us; I used that example all my life. I forgot about Pollock, and it became Friedan's cemetery. I put a small stone on her cement marker and thanked her, expressed my gratitude.

But what structure did I have now? Only a fear of Covid.

Eddie makes it through the emergency surgery on his left leg. He is in the hospital for two weeks. St. Vincent in Santa Fe; not always reputable, but they are making a great effort, and he has a good stay—and cannot wait to get out. He calls once from the hospital. "No one can visit during Covid," he repeats.

"Okay," I say.

"Okay," he says. He's drugged. The call is short.

After two weeks home, I drive out along St. Francis and then make a left on a dirt road. Mary rolls Eddie out in his wheelchair and then she steps back into the house. I know he is in good hands. Mary used to be a nurse. Their younger son in Dallas drove out to help Mary when Eddie first came home. He's pale, thinner, hair disheveled, and seems fragile. A big man, often silent in public, he can talk one-on-one. I didn't expect him to be so diminished. His surgery on the broken bone has to heal completely before he can put weight on it; his world, too, is limited now, to his home.

I leave after fifteen minutes. Eddie is tired. For now, my Covid buddy is gone.

Gnats, flies, moths stir all around me. I watch a monarch twitter in the juniper branches. I look past the hedge to a cloud and experience this unalleviated ennui, this feeling again and again of being a housewife in the Fifties in the unforgiving suburbs.

Each day waking, going nowhere. In a quiet, almost dull moment, there is air, a lightness. It's early morning, shadows long across the cement portal floor, an opening, a leap happens: *This must have been how my mother felt?* For the first time ever I am flooded with understanding—no, I'll admit it, *compassion*—a softness for the woman who gave birth to me in a Brooklyn hospital, unconscious, drugged, my father asleep on the sofa in his in-laws' apartment. Only my grandparents sat in the waiting room, alive with hope.

My mother had been dead for fifteen years by this point. I'd done plenty of psychological work around her and fully understood the dynamics of my childhood, but I could never take the big step to *feel* love for her. Here, because my life is at a dead stop, I am given a gift, saturated with emotion for my mother. I miss her so. My hands motion in the thin dry air, gesturing to her, not even sure she knew that I had hated her. She mattered deeply to me, and I feel the poignancy of the years passed.

From a very young age, I was on my own, even though my mother was a housewife and did not have a job outside the home. I had to figure out on the first day of first grade which bus to take and what to do at twelve years old when blood fell between my legs. She rarely talked to me or asked anything about me, but she shopped mercilessly. Big bargain stores were sprouting all over suburban Long Island. Fortunoff's, Ohrbach's, Loehmann's. No driving distance was too far. She'd also dip into Saks, Abraham & Straus, and Lord & Taylor for price comparisons. Those fancy department stores were a lovely balm for her, the soft carpets, the put-together saleswomen, the perfume spray atomizers, the original escalators gliding softly up to the next floor of apparel—anything you can imagine for your body. My little sister, three years younger, caught the fever. They shopped together.

I never did anything with my mother but sit in dressing rooms, reading a book, or in the back seat of the Buick, watching the click of exits go by. To placate me when I whined, "Can't we go home?" she offered an ice cream after we shopped.

Sweets became my consolation. At Howard Johnson's I pressed to go further than the coffee ice cream scoop in a silver dish. "How about hot fudge?" A leap, a break in the sullen routine. In those days HoJo's could really lay on the accoutrements. The dark fudge glowed in the neon ceiling lights and coagulated into a semihard shape curved on top of the scoop. All my female ten-year-old desire bent into that dish. It became destiny, goal, raison d'être in my feeble life. No dreams for us but to get married, so your husband could provide the means to continue shopping. I was not a good prospect for this, but I saw no other.

When my mother was thirteen years old, she weighed 180 pounds. She attended one of the big public high schools in Brooklyn, either Erasmus or Tilden. They were all famous for one kind of sport or another. In gym class they weighed each student and shouted out the number to the notetaker across the room. My mother dreaded that first day of gym each year.

She did slim down, and right after high school she found a job selling cosmetics in Macy's.

My mother was beautiful. Thick black curly hair, black eyes, and the darkest eyebrows shading those eyes. And her smile, big-toothed, hearty. I'd watch her apply the reddest

Revlon lipstick. Once after she ate an Oreo, a crumb lingered at the corner of her mouth.

I regarded her every move in total secret concentration, though I hardly existed for her. Eventually, my pain and longing was so intense, I transmuted it into rage. I'd sit in the back seat of the tan car as we navigated to another shopping mall and wanted so badly to put my hands from behind around her neck and choke her. Sometimes, we'd head to grocery stores, and she'd speak about the half-price sale on cheese at Waldbaum's. Trader Joe's would have spun her into ecstasy, if they'd existed back then.

She had two brothers. She arrived nine years after them, a surprise to her immigrant parents who were finally getting a foothold in America. Their poultry business was a success; it produced a living for the family. I surmise she didn't get much attention, but she had the relief of digging into her mother's cooking. Being overweight in this immigrant haven was expected, a sign that you could afford to be well-fed. But, oh, put her outside the comfortable parameters of home and into a gym class, and all the shame of years of Eastern European oppression weighed down that scale. And forget athletics. No one in the shtetls that my grandparents escaped was allowed to own land, to farm, to build their bodies. Caught in overpopulated ghettos, a living was made by the one thing Jews were allowed to do: lend money and collect interest, a task beneath the Gentiles.

My grandparents put all their hopes and dreams into

the eldest son, Emmanuel. He would become a medical doctor, the holiest of holies. When he couldn't perform the required push-ups to graduate from the public high school, Grandma met with the gym teacher. These gym teachers wielded a lot of power. She hinted that some other boy could take Mendel's place and do the required athletic demonstrations. She would be happy to support the young man's effort—and, of course, the teacher.

My uncle Manny went to the University of Rochester for undergraduate school. During the cold winters of up-state New York, my grandmother sent long kosher salamis and roasted chickens that my uncle shared with room-mates and hung out the windows on strong twine in place of refrigeration. She also sent up boxes of raspberry butter cookies she baked herself.

When he became a doctor, my grandparents were complete. He was the god in the family. For my mother, shopping took the place of her own chance at education or dreams, disillusion, whatever it was she carried to the clothes swinging on racks in the department stores.

My mother ingested sleeping pills every night, easily available from her physician older brother. It must have been why morning after morning she seemed relieved when she woke me for school and I complained of a head-ache or sore throat. She immediately gave in and wandered back to her bedroom and I lost another day of learning and interaction with people my own age.

On other days she made me repeatedly the same tuna

sandwich, but did not drain the oil, so by lunchtime the white bread was so soaked it was almost transparent. I'd dump the sandwich into the big garbage bin in the cafeteria and instead buy day after day a Drake's round coffee cake, crumbles on top, wrapped straight from the distributor in cellophane. I don't even know where I would have come up with the change for the Drake's.

My grandmother must have had the second shift with us: breakfast and delicious dinners on TV trays as we were mesmerized by TV shows. Potatoes mashed with real butter (no margarine, even in those Fifties). Grandma believed in the real thing. The potato pulp put back in the nutritious skin. A side of peas or string beans were served, thanks to frozen Birds Eye. What a name. Were the birds watching? Chicken, baked in an orange sauce, a bottle of French salad dressing in a jar poured over, the recipe found in *Newsday*.

Eddie was right. My mother never had much interest in her older daughter, nor much care for her younger daughter, though my sister took on the shopping addiction gene, and later transferred that to smoking marijuana, long before it was legal.

I was born in 1948, just when the concentration camps were being revealed, the emaciated skeletons in striped pajamas staring at the camera and at you in newspaper photos. No way could my parents comprehend or digest this news. My father had fought in World War II, but knew nothing about the camps until later.

I suspect this unconscious pain of the war, which they

did not discuss, was poured undiluted into my veins and my sister's. It created a generation that, not knowing why we felt crazy, smoked weed and discovered LSD, a way to break open our vision, to find some larger purpose and connection, to skip over the deadness of the Fifties that covered so much suffering and disillusionment.

In every small town in Europe that I've been to, there are memorials to the people they lost, a recognition of broken lives. But in the US, we marched on and were told we were victorious and great; we fed on progress, proud of a bomb we created that could destroy two whole Japanese cities.

Looking back, I felt my father could carry sorrow, could hold dismay in his body, but my mother was always nervous, *aggravated*. So many tensions switch-crossed her psyche, but she had no way to face or understand them.

I wonder now if the pogroms, that dreaded persecution, officially sanctioned, especially in Eastern Europe for over a thousand years toward Jews, leaked from her parents into my mother unbeknownst and unconsciously from being of first generation in the US. Except for shopping, she seemed so timid.

She married my father on the rebound. She'd been engaged to the next-door neighbor in the brownstone in Brooklyn. Eddie Smith. When he returned from the war, he broke up with her. From time to time she mentioned him. The last was when she was in her early nineties— "Natli, I hear those computers can find anything. Do you think they could find Eddie Smith? Is he still alive? Where is he?"

She used to scream from the top of the stairs, mostly about my father's inattention. I'd duck into the bedroom I shared with my sister, lie down on the bed, and bury my head under the pillow. My grandparents in the next bedroom retired to the room they shared, and my father stared numbly at the TV in my parents' bedroom. My little sister would run and grab her leg, sobbing. My mother used it as fuel: "See what you've done to upset Rita." This extreme yelling was not emotional communication. It was another way of saying nothing, shutting us all down even more. Even when I went away to college, I could hear her screams in my head.

I realize now she was lonely; her childhood was sacrificed to the glory of the eldest son realizing physician-hood. Like me, she had received little attention, born as an afterthought in her mother's later life. But still, she and my grandmother were close. When she married my father, they moved into my grandparents' apartment; and when my father bought the Aero Tavern with his war buddy Frank Leone, my grandparents moved out with us to Long Island.

By the time my grandparents were out in the suburbs, what they deemed "the country," they were broke. Their second son had moved to Miami to ward off terrible psoriasis. He failed at one business after another, and my grandparents kept bailing him out. The last time they helped him, my grandmother had to pull out the diamond studs from her long earlobes and hand them over to the hockshop.

In Farmingdale, on the border of Nassau and Suffolk Counties, my grandparents easily fit into the small bedroom, because they had so little. But with the verve and inspiration of immigrants, they dived into suburban life. Grandpa hung shirts and pajamas on the clothesline in the backyard and pushed the manual mower back and forth across the new lawn, adjusted the position of the sprinklers, spraying back and forth across the azaleas, tulips, rhododendron, and my father's favorite, the mimosa, which rapidly umbrellaed out across the front lawn and sprouted pink exotic flowers like pom-poms every spring.

My grandmother took over the cooking, ironing, bedmaking. All to free my mother to go on her manic shopping sprees, buying and then returning purchases, probably, I realize now, to get away from her parents. My mother had thinned down to size 12, but she never felt okay about her body. She was continually on a diet, fighting the pleasure of ice cream, but then standing at the freezer and spooning it in late at night. I don't ever remember her plainly enjoying a meal.

It was from my father that I learned the diversity of eating, the pure abandoned pleasure of Bing cherries, pistachios, my grandmother's chicken, cherry vanilla ice cream, even boiled-to-death cauliflower. He was skinny before he was introduced to the Edelsteins but cared not at all how big he became. Bulking up actually helped him as bartender and bouncer in the tavern he owned and where he worked nights.

After my father's death, alone her last eight years, my mother lived in the small cottage in Florida—my father's paradise—that they moved into when he retired in his early sixties. He had sold the tavern, but he still talked long distance on the phone to the "boys" and the longtime waitress. He'd been at the bar for thirty years. Slowly that connection, too, faded as he faded. A big man whose muscles became flabby, though he still made a racer's dive into the condo pool that had visible signs posted to the fence: NO DIVING. He'd been a champion swimmer in high school.

When I visited my mother in Florida, I was shocked at how she had aged. I still carried the young image of her with black hair in the latest coif. Getting old was not a part of my awareness of her. I was stuck, frozen with so much old rage and disconnection, torn between these hard emotions and my need to care for an old woman, dependent as she always had been, with little skill to help herself. She'd never in her whole life been alone.

"Call me. Call me," she repeated on the phone.

"Once a week isn't enough?" I said, cringing.

"When are you coming to visit?"

"Mom, I was there last month." The trip to Florida from New Mexico takes all day—the hour drive to Albuquerque, the plane switch in Dallas/Fort Worth, the car rental in the West Palm Beach airport, and then the half-hour drive to my mother's Buttonwood senior development in Green Acres. The two-hour Eastern time switch put me in the dark at arrival—and I had left that morning from Santa Fe in the dark. That visit was also in the middle of a lot of work travel, but I tried to see her at least three times a year.

Each time I went I promised myself it would be good. Soon after I arrived, the anger I never could afford to feel before enveloped me with no outlet. I certainly couldn't express this to an old woman. I was torn, wanting to care for her and despising her, the visit igniting what I tried to contain. Why go? I couldn't not go. I was a good Jewish girl. From a distance I had great empathy. She wouldn't leave the house unless my sister or I took her out. She was afraid of falling.

When my sister visited, they frolicked in the plenitude of shopping in the land of palm trees and humidity, the air conditioners blasting in those box stores. My mother became alive again in familiar territory. They even found a discount fish restaurant, and there were always senior discounts for having dinner at 4 P.M.

I refused to take her to those places. I'd gone all my childhood and hated it. I drove her to the beach. We sat on cement benches and stared out at the vast ocean.

As those years after my father's death clicked by, I comprehended the pain I still carried from my youth. I was working hard in therapy, but I couldn't confront her as I had done with my father years ago. I was too late. Soon she would be ninety. At the beginning of an April visit, I decided to try a new tactic. I thought I'd begin with generosity of purse and hope that generosity of heart would follow.

"Mom, there's a small clothes shop in Palm Beach. I think there is a sale." I still couldn't bear to go to the big discount stores. Her face lit up. The second day of a visit is still early; all is new and possible.

We loaded her walker into the trunk of the Chevrolet rental and off we went.

"I didn't know those kinds of places had much sales," she mused as we drove past old tropical architecture. "Probably only a rack, a trick to get us in."

I parallel parked right in front of the store, opened her side, lifted out the walker, held open the glass store door.

She hobbled on the sidewalk, lifting and placing the walker. Then she paused at the entrance, assessing the territory. The boutique was empty of any other customers.

I walked up to the saleswoman behind the cash register and whispered, though by now my mother was hard of hearing, "Tell her please that everything is greatly reduced, even to ten and twenty dollars. Don't worry, I'll pay the real price."

The saleswoman, in sturdy shoes, immaculate makeup, and tweezed eyebrows, went over to my mother.

In a quick glance my mother took in her light cashmere sweater and straight skirt.

"You are lucky. Anything you purchase today is

reduced to a mere twenty or thirty dollars." She swept her hand across the racks of clothes. The saleswoman couldn't comprehend *ten dollars.*

My mother beamed. Her left eye had only about 10 percent of its vision after a failed cataract operation, but suddenly it seemed that her sight was restored. She pushed the walker out of the way and dived into the racks, flipping through blouses, sweaters, jackets, like a professional cardplayer in Las Vegas.

I was delighted to see her so energetic. I told her I'd pay for anything she wanted.

She chose a green blouse, a button-down blue sweater, and two cotton jackets. We stood at the cashier station. The saleswoman slipped behind the counter. I handed her my Visa card and raised my eyebrows, but she was ahead of me. "Your purchase comes to eighty dollars, but because your mother is so sweet, I'm taking off an additional ten dollars," she said loudly.

My mother nodded, pleased with the discount. The walker was still by the door. I signed the receipt for three hundred and thirty dollars.

"Let's go to Hamburger Heaven, it's around the corner," I said as we settled into the car. "It's an old casual diner with lots of windows, booths, and good food. Let's share a malt."

"I really shouldn't," she said, "but okay."

We also ordered a single hamburger and fries. Her digestion was slow in her late eighties.

A woman in blue nursing scrubs, a businessman with his white sleeves rolled up, and an older retired couple were at the counter. Across the aisle, one woman in a red sweater with sequins on the bodice dipped her head over a bowl of minestrone.

In walked a tall woman with a poodle—exactly the ideal personality imagined in Palm Beach. A heavy diamond on her left hand, gold studs in her ears. A violet/blue/red lipstick. Her long hair coiffed in a chignon. She was mostly ignored by this crowd, but my mother instinctively snapped her head around as the blonde entered, and her sight seemed suddenly 20/20. "Those pants are an Irish plaid—very expensive. And her shirt is fine cotton from Wanamaker's."

I hadn't even noticed the plaid. I realized for the first time that my mother had a gift. In another life she might have been a designer. Who knew the possibilities of her talent? I also realized that I inherited her love of beauty, although what we considered beautiful was so different.

The waitress placed the plates in front of us. "Your mother is so cute."

My mother preened and shook her head. "I'm old."

She did look lovely. Her eyebrows were still thick and black, and her curly hair never turned all gray. She was small now, and too thin.

She started to tell me about a slight from a woman down the block where she lives.

"You want ketchup?" I cut her off. I couldn't bear her hurts.

She enjoyed the shake and took a few bites of the hamburger. Driving home with her hand on her stomach, she said, "I shouldn't have. I'll be sick."

She sat in the big blue Naugahyde chair that my father used to sit in, in front of the TV—which was always on, though she couldn't see or hear it—and fingered the new cardigan.

"Who are they kidding? This isn't worth twenty dollars. They probably got it for a dollar. A bargain? Humph." She ran her hand over the buttons, complaining, "They are on the wrong side." She skewered up her mouth. "We should return it."

All week I counted the days: Tuesday, Wednesday, Thursday, Friday—I was leaving Sunday. She found one thing after another that was wrong with the bargain clothes and how they ripped me off. She complained every day.

I said nothing. The old rage was too volatile. I was afraid: it could bring down the house. I walked back and forth to the condo pool where no residents appeared. It was May in Florida and too hot for the elderly who lived there. They stayed hidden in their air-conditioned units with the blinds down.

Saturday night I took her out for dinner. I was almost out of there.

We drove back and I didn't say a word. She reached

over from the passenger seat and touched my arm. I cringed. I didn't think she saw. "You're so cold," she said.

Finally, I broke. "You've complained all week about the clothes. You never even thanked me!" I yelled. I was so glad I hadn't spouted all the resentments of childhood. I kept it to this one thing. I told her the real prices.

"No?" Her mouth hung open. "Nat-a-lee," she pronounced all three syllables, rather than *Natli*. "I don't believe you."

"Yes." We were almost home. "I'll show you."

I charged into the back bedroom and rifled through my already packed bag and found the receipt under a swimsuit.

She was standing by her blue chair, holding on to the back of it. I handed her the bill with the list of clothing, the prices, tax, total. "Here," I said, victorious.

She bent her head, reading slowly. She looked up at me. "You love me this much?"

Shocked at her response, I simply replied, "Yes." Love transmuted into clothes? We had never been so naked with each other.

This will be it, I thought. *She's too old.* All the pain of my childhood I will have to carry in my own arms, never to be able to share with her. I didn't even quite understand what happened. She never thought I loved her? Needed her?

Our first move out on Long Island was to Levittown. I was still not school-age, but one morning the kids on the corner ganged up on me. I ran home crying, and there she was, vacuuming. She did not let me in and instead screamed through the screen door, "Don't I have enough aggravation?"

At four, at five, at six years old I acted competent, to please her. I asked nothing of her, hoping that would win her love. She always seemed overwhelmed, worried, and if she didn't have to deal with me, if I didn't bother her, maybe she'd notice me. Of course, as a young child I did not reason or scheme a tactic. I was trying in my young way a plausible response to win a mother's love.

As an adult in my fifties, I once wrote to her, "How come you never helped me with homework, helped me pick out my school clothes? All through high school and junior high I put on the same wool plaid pleated skirt and blue sweater. You never talked to me."

In her beautiful handwriting (it seems beautiful to me now, when she will never write again): "Oh, I was a softie, always administering to Grandma and your father. I should have checked in on you."

It all made sense. I'd suffered terribly as a child, but I now grasped her life, her own disappointment and suffering. It was a small miracle. My mother and I were no longer separate; how filled with gratitude and also how I grieved that she was gone. Finally, in my own later years, my heart was open to her. This was a quiet victory in an American land of great turmoil and a mysterious disease called Covid.

PART II

THE CEMETERY

I HAD BEEN invited a year before the pandemic to a month-long writer's residency in Port Townsend, Washington, through Centrum, an art organization. The time was coming up soon. I had been looking forward to it. They would give me a cabin to live and write in. No demands. I also had a residency there three years before while working on *Three Simple Lines,* a book about haiku.

The town was on a peninsula, so wherever I went, the sea was in my vision, the exact opposite from dry, high altitude northern New Mexico. A window over the sink where I washed my single fork, two spoons, two plates, and one cup allowed me to look out at the view. Always a Zen student at heart, I loved that austere life. And there was plentiful fresh, inexpensive fish. In that first residency, I met a woman from Lincoln, Nebraska, who had a Ph.D. in English literature. I knew Nebraska, I told her, and we began a hiking friendship.

While I was in Port Townsend that first time, I took a

ferry across the Strait of Juan de Fuca from Port Angeles to Victoria, a quaint city in Canada, and met a friend from Vancouver there. After the three-day excursion, I drove back, the big leaf maples, quaking aspen, the alder, all blazing against the green of Douglas fir, cedar, and hemlock, in the height of autumn along the highway. Then right up in front dropped the full moon. I know moons rise, but plop! There it was, looking straight at me in the deep dark sky. I was the only car on the road moving east, back to my own destiny in my bungalow in old Fort Worden. I had one more week left.

Port Angeles, where I returned on the ferry, was the home of Raymond Carver (1938–1988), the great writer who contributed to revitalizing the short story form in the Eighties. His work focused on sadness, the lower middle class, marginalized people, and his relief and gratitude. He died too young, at only fifty years old. He was buried overlooking the water.

When I visited, I could feel, even years later, the pain, longing, and heartbreak at his gravesite, where his wife, the poet Tess Gallagher, put her name and had space for her eventual burial next to his, though she was still young and would be alive for many years. They met at a writer's conference in Dallas in 1977, and he began his second life with her in '78 after he stopped his heavy drinking. Six weeks before he died, they married. Before that they lived together, and anyone who met them said their love was palpable.

His tombstone was big, flat black marble with two of his poems inscribed on top, "Gravy" and "Late Fragment." He'd been able to maintain his sobriety after abusing alcohol during years of raising kids, miscellaneous jobs, and his first early marriage. He called Tess not only his love but his muse. Also attached to the flat gravestone was a small bench of the same dark material, where you could sit and write in a small spiral notebook tied to the bench leg. A lot of writing in the beginning of the book was by Tess. It felt private; I didn't read it. I'd never been to such an elaborate grave. The disappointment was evident. They were so young and full of passion.

That fall I had seen salmon going back upstream to their natal home where they first tasted the sweet cold water of their birth; and though they might have traveled for up to two years in the big salty Pacific, all the way even to Alaskan waters, when it was time to spawn, to lay their eggs, the ocean temperatures, the salinity, the angle of the sun and magnetic fields guided them back home. For two weeks they stayed at the mouth of the river, adjusting again to freshwater. They knew the direction and the route by taste, finally swimming upstream, jumping high out of the water to overtake rough waterfalls and eddies, their fins pushing through the air, parts of their bodies already decomposing, giving themselves over to the cycle of life.

Years before, my friend Wendy in California told me of this salmon journey, but I never believed her. She had a vast imagination, and I loved the story. But here it was before me, the huge determination, the gathering in quiet pools, attempting again and again the fast stream that was running against them. I had witnessed this with my own eyes.

Driving home from Canada, a thought shot through me: this is the happiest I have ever been.

But that was three years ago. *I should cancel the residency,* I thought. That would be the Covid-sensible thing to do. It was inconceivable to fly, and driving seemed an impossibility, so many miles. (The vaccines were not even out yet.) I hadn't driven long distance since I was young.

One evening during dinner, out of the blue, my girlfriend, Yu-kwan, offered, "I'll drive you to that residency. I'll fly home and you can have the car."

"I'm that bad, huh?"

She nodded. "Even your old friend Annie said she never saw you like this." I could not snap out of my inert misery.

I reached for the last of the spinach. I took a big gulp of water. "Okay," I said with hesitation. I couldn't imagine what I would work on. I no longer felt like a writer. I was a fake.

I'm in the passenger seat. We are headed northwest, but are subject to peculiar navigation through industrial farming and barren land. Yu-kwan has taken her cue from Google, who doesn't know anything about New Mexico or beauty. Google is just trying to shave off three or four extra miles on the first day of our journey. It doesn't even signal when you've passed into another state.

I hate Google and the mechanized world, but I keep my mouth shut. I feel grateful that Yu-kwan has taken over navigation. All I did was throw a few notebooks and some clothes into the car trunk. We left for our journey very early in the morning. Yu-kwan, who fears getting lost, only learned to drive seven years ago when she moved out from New York City. We are a ridiculous couple. I adore getting lost. We are driving this first night to Salt Lake City. I hate passing through Moab without stopping— they have a great bookstore—and then through the Canyonlands. But since I'm numb and disconnected, desire has left me. We'll stay two nights, a whole day of rest, in Utah's main city.

When we get to the hotel, we wipe down every surface with sanitized wipes.

In late afternoon I eat an orange that we bought at a grocer near the hotel. I had picked up a map of the Northwest states before we left. I unfold it on the bed. Yu-kwan has never looked at a map, much less trusted it for directions. I follow my finger north along the highway.

"We go through the bottom of Idaho," I surmise.

She is reading a book. She turns her head. "Yes."

"Hmm, never imagined I'd be in that state." I get up to

find my reading glasses. Pick up the map again. "There's a place about two hours out of our way, more north, that I've always wanted to go to."

"Let's go, then. We have plenty of time." We'd given ourselves a week for driving.

"No, we can't. Too far," I say. She's gone back to her book. I trace my finger over and over the detour. Should we do it? The drive already is so long. Really, four hours out of our way—two there, then two back. "Maybe we can stay overnight?"

She doesn't hear me.

I get my iPhone, which I dislike, but find useful, and look up hotels there. It's well past Labor Day, and a hotel pops up with a 25 percent price reduction.

I try every which way to talk myself out of it as I call the hotel and the phone rings. I have visited graves of writers and painters I've loved, but this was the white whale, the great catch, the one from my early writing life when I struggled to understand how it was done.

"Two nights?" I say.

"Yes, why you coming? This is a remote place and summer is over," Henry—he's told me his name—asks.

I tell him.

"The only reason to come," he says. "You know, we are in walking distance." I give him my Visa to hold the room.

Yu-kwan is fast asleep, one of her thunderous naps. No sound can break in, but I know she will love the idea, anything for me to wake out of deepfreeze—and I feel it. I'm a little excited. I pace the room. Really, I've wanted to go there for at least thirty years, but Idaho always was where I was never going, never had another reason.

We pull into the hotel late afternoon the next day. I've been driving for many hours. We've dropped Google.

"Let's go tomorrow. It's late. I'm tired," Yu-kwan says.

"You have to be kidding?"

"Go ahead. I'll unpack."

I run down the two blocks of sidewalk. The light is dimming, sun almost setting behind the coffee shop and athletic store across the street, both closed.

I get to the cemetery. I see a cross, a Jewish star, green grass, trees. It's getting colder. I thought I would be magnetized to his grave. The cemetery has no closing hours, no fence, no limit around it.

I call Henry. "Where is it?"

"See two pines, really close together? Only one grave can fit between."

I glance around. "There's tons of pines—wait. I think—" I hang up, walk up slowly, almost straight in front of me.

Flat, rectangular cement, large enough a man can be buried under it, just the name and the date. Nothing about books or winning the Nobel.

ERNEST MILLER HEMINGWAY 1899–1961

Hemingway shot himself in the head at sixty-two years old. He'd had electric shock treatment two separate times back in Rochester, Minnesota, at the Mayo Clinic. He said they took his heart. He struggled near the end to write a memoir of his early years in Paris, *A Moveable Feast,* one of my very favorites. I studied it carefully to learn how to write. One time in my early thirties I walked to every café in the book, sat down in each, ordered a kir royale—not something he drank—sipped it and looked around, imagining a different time, a different life. Café de Lilas, Le Select—places in Paris didn't change that much. That was their charm. It was late on a Wednesday; all of them were mostly empty. It was safe in the Eighties for a young woman to walk the streets at night alone.

This memoir, his last book, was about the early sweet years with his first wife and young son. Even then, I could feel the drinking, the drive to get to a café, walking down the Paris streets, to be near alcohol. Even if he didn't have his first glass till after he wrote, the thrill was all around him—at the other tables, behind the bar in glittering bottles. It was also when he wrote deep into Michigan when he had the freedom of European distance. He called it "transplanting yourself" and yes, sometimes he did drink as he wrote. But it was the writing distance that impressed me as a young woman. It meant if I could get distance from my childhood, I could write about what haunted me.

I sit down on the pine root to the left of the grave, settle in, and talk to him. By now, even his bones are dust, almost sixty years later; but where else would I find him? Let's not think that the coffin caved in long ago, though I'm sure it did. I want finally to tell him of the Spanish train I rode through the yellow hills in the countryside, reading *Death in the Afternoon,* about bullfighting. How I admired his bravery to know death. Death had always followed him. His father, then also one of his brothers and a sister, committed suicide. I don't tell him that I didn't admire his killing so many wild animals in Africa—hundreds, their beautiful spotted or tan or striped coats lined up next to each other—just for the sport, for the taste of blood.

I talk about my dilemma: how I can't write anymore. It all seems useless. I tell him about my trip to Cuba for the short time President Obama opened that country to US visitors, how I climbed the stairs to the studio where he wrote *Old Man and the Sea,* the book that brought him out of slow obscurity, the US being the most fickle about books; the book that tilted the balance, that won him the biggest prize, the Nobel in Literature, even though he scoffed at the honor, wasn't well enough to travel to Sweden. He asked John Cabot, the US Ambassador to Sweden at the time, to read his brief, odd acceptance speech, afraid he'd never write again. Many writers feared winning this prize and not writing again.

A long line of people waited to climb those stairs in Cuba to peek in where that slim book hummed in his body and brain. In his studio was a simple table with a typewriter in the middle of the room and a small bookcase against the wall, almost nothing else.

I sobbed uncontrollably when I saw this. What is it to be a human being, to have vision inside you, to create true beauty, like a hum of bees, and then the other life, too—destroying himself, his cruelty to wives, mental illness, his family's history, and always the drink? Finally lost in your own illusions and pain.

I tell him that, during Covid, isolated and numb, I tried to use reason. I told myself: you've written enough, you are tired, you missed out on a lot of other things with your dedication. Let's have some of the pleasure normal people enjoy. *Normal* was the key word. Exactly how do they enjoy their life? It was too late for me to have children, but I had a partner and a house. Okay, let's begin by healthy dinners every night, checking the roof for any repairs it might need, planting a few more trees, trying to get rid of the moths that were eating my sweaters.

We watched Netflix.

"You didn't have Netflix," I explain, "stories in series. I couldn't wait to see the next one. Sometimes we watched three in a row, walked around blurry-eyed the next day, waiting for evening and the next installment. Several weeks passed. Then I thought, so this is it? This is a life?"

Time ground me down. A few months of "normality" was okay. No, it wasn't. The news on the radio, in papers, was unbearable. The inequity, unemployment, poverty, fear, the blame of the virus on Asian Americans. Some days I snapped the dial on the radio to off while I drove my car to a park; other times I pulled over and listened. Myanmar,

North Korea, Iraq, the starvation, the white supremacy, proliferation of guns, all piling on, one news announcement after another. *Stop!* I wanted to run in the street and flag cars down. *Do you hear this? How can we go on?*

I'd ask myself, how can I hold this, bear it, how can I help? Blinders were being ripped off.

I didn't want to be a writer anymore. I didn't want to teach writing. But when I stopped both, a chasm opened. Endless forms of suffering and ignorance slapped me in the face. I'd lost any purpose.

I really am on a roll, telling him everything. I'd been lonely, I'd been terribly lonely as a kid. Covid creates that kind of isolation. I can picture the darkness I felt on the New York suburban streets. I talk to him, even if he can't talk back.

A Pontiac pulls up at the empty parking lot. Two women come out. One walks right toward me.

"This, his grave?" The one with a blue cardigan, sleeves pushed up to her elbows, points.

I nod.

She swivels her head. "Here," she yells across the grave markers.

They both stand, arms at their sides.

"Where you from?" I'm still sitting on the tree root, trying to be friendly.

"Detroit."

"I lived in Detroit once in my early twenties." It doesn't grab them.

The woman on the left has thick ankles and wears a T-shirt that says "Kill" with a can exploding.

"Ever read his books?" I venture.

Both shake their heads. "We just wanted to see the grave," the one on the right, with clipped short hair and a streak of pink, offers.

Then, just like that, they turn on their heels and walk back to their car. One of them has a lightning tattoo on her calf. Not even a goodbye.

I continue, prattling on in the cemetery in the creeping dark. Here he is, after all—after all these years. I have a shawl wrapped around me and a streetlight nearby turns on.

"I dried up after fifteen books," I tell him. "One came after the other, crowded to get in line. Then nothing but the empty days on the portal and Covid burning up the sidewalks. My last book was about *haiku*." I quickly drop that subject, afraid Hemingway didn't care about haiku.

I'm sure I repeated myself.

Finally, I unwind as much as I can, and then there is nothing. But it is dumb clear, even with no revelation—it comes from me, not him: *Write anyway.* No ecstatic understanding. No big epiphany.

I walk back to the hotel in the gloomy dark. But write what? The mantle was back on. I thought I might get a break—a new career, new passion. Race car driving?

What did you think? I ask myself. *You went to a writer for help.*

I was ignorant of a writer's path when I was young and still hoped to escape, but I was married to it. Visiting Hemingway only drove that home. Like other marriages, you don't know what you're getting into until you stay and meet it, moment by moment.

I think of the words of Suzuki Roshi, the Japanese Zen master, when someone asked him what enlightenment was: *Seeing one thing through to the end.* I guess that fit for anything you seriously take on.

Hemingway, in his terrible craziness and suffering, made an effort to write to the end with *A Moveable Feast,* even though it needed editing later by his wife Mary.

The next day, the director of the community library gives me a tour of the house in Ketchum that Ernest and Mary lived in together for two years. We stand in the foyer where he shot himself, pause a moment, then move on. The living room feels familiar after seeing his Cuba home and also the one in Key West. Uncluttered, low couch, big windows. The furniture of that era. Mary had made the garage into an apartment after her husband died.

We spend at least two hours at the house. The librarian, a native Idahoan, wants her state recognized for its literary accomplishments. I mention Tom Spanbauer, who was born and raised in Pocatello, Idaho. His novels are full of his hometown. (I don't mention he was glad to get away.)

Mostly, Hemingway stood and wrote on the top of a tall clothes bureau because he had a bad back. A curled,

Scotch-taped print of a Cézanne landscape is on the bedroom closet door. In *A Moveable Feast,* after writing in a café, he'd visit the Paris art museums. He wanted to write like Cézanne painted.

A year after this trip, in 2021, a Hemingway documentary will come out by Lynn Novick and Ken Burns, revealing hard-to-accept incidents about the author. The one that burns itself into my brain was when he was courting his last wife, Mary, in Paris. She received a letter from her ex-husband, and Ernest went into a jealous rage, grabbed the letter, tore it up, threw it into the toilet in their top-floor hotel room, and then machine-gunned the toilet. The ceilings of the rooms below dripped with water for days.

"Leave him now!" I will scream, watching the film. But she didn't—the pull of fame must have been strong.

After he died, Mary spent most of the twenty years she had left in Manhattan; but as I departed the cemetery, I noticed the same large flat marker as Ernest's to the lower left of the plot. It was hers. Only one could fit between the pines.

And to the right, lower down, was the marker for Hemingway's first son from his first marriage, who lived in Paris with his parents when he was young. They called him Bumby.

PART III

CENTRUM RESIDENCY

We have reached a hastier and superficial rhythm, now that we
believe we are in touch with a greater amount of people, more
people, more countries. This is the illusion which might cheat
us of being in touch deeply with the one breathing next to us.
The dangerous time when mechanical voices, radios, tele-
phones, take the place of human intimacies, and the concept
of being in touch with millions brings a greater and greater
poverty in intimacy and human vision.
—Anaïs Nin (fourth journal, 1944)

WE LEFT IDAHO late the next morning and headed
straight for Seattle, pulling into downtown early evening—
almost everything was shut, windows of sports equipment
and department stores boarded up. People roved the streets,
a few screaming. The sounds bounced off empty structures.
I assumed most of them were homeless, with shopping carts,
tents set up against buildings. Pike Place Market, usually

lively, was half closed. Elliott Bay Book Company had just reopened. You were allowed a half hour inside, eight people permitted at a time; their coffee shop and bathrooms were closed.

The next morning, Yu-kwan flew Alaskan Airlines nonstop back to Albuquerque. Just as I kissed her goodbye, an image came to me from two years before. She is in a one-piece bathing suit with some frill at the bodice, her thin legs tucked under her, sitting sideways on that gentle sand slope that rises up just before a beach's descent into water. A wave had just crested, broken, thundered and retreated. She won't go in. She can't swim. In her childhood in Hong Kong, there were no swimming lessons, no bike riding either, nor table tennis, nor volleyball. Forget that—she didn't learn to brush her teeth till she was ten. Before that age, she said she would have eaten the toothpaste, she was so hungry. But here she is at a later time. I come out of surfing a wave and walk over, sand filling my suit, and I bend to kiss her. She lifts her face, stretches her neck; and in that moment, I am overcome with a love I've never felt before. This isn't quite passion; it's different, as though I stepped out of Earth's gravitational pull and was absorbed into the sun's light. I feel a tenderness inexplicable, outside time. Our relationship, just then, like the waves, crashed all old ideas, the rules of bonding I was raised with.

Now she was gone, and I drove onto the 11:50 A.M. ferry to Bainbridge, then off the ramp, and proceeded an hour over two bridges on five different roads till I arrived at Fort Worden, an old military and naval base, currently a park and art center.

I park my car outside of the cabin and unload. *I can do this,* I said to myself, choosing the back bedroom out of four disheveled ones. I had not forgotten the people being removed from apartments all over the country because they could not pay their rent during this pandemic. Here I was blessed to have four bedrooms, even if their mattresses were lumpy.

I never realized how hungry I was to be completely alone, my cells gulping the solitude like protein. I was brought up that being alone was shameful. Either you were weird, or you were sick. "Jews stay together." It was how we survived. It was drummed into me. Solitude for me was always a guilty pleasure. This time I devoured it whole, no reservations.

I drove to the Port Townsend co-op—a substantial one—and loaded up. Eggs, yogurt with marionberries— I'd never heard of them before—fresh salmon, Humboldt Fog cheese from California with a blue ash vein running down the center, salt, pepper, olive oil. Nothing was provided but one pot, one pan, two plates, two forks and a single spoon. I loved this austerity and knew it from three years before. Two thin white towels, a few slabs of white nondescript soap, no shampoo. The bare bones of it made you want to write, to draw thoughts out of you.

Alas, all I had was an inkling of a topic to write about: why I hated the internet, one of the last talks I gave to a weeklong class, including what to do instead of playing all day with your devices. Rather than throwing balled-up papers at me, I noticed they listened.

My co-teacher pulled me aside—he was twenty years younger—and said, "We are all ashamed of the addiction."

Really?

But what did I really know about computers? Their use was growing during the painful, empty time of Covid. People reached out to each other while the world closed down. Zoom (zip-zap) was the only way to see each other. The connection to friends and family seemed to grow; even those who formerly couldn't bear their relatives were suddenly tight and Zooming with them like mad. People realized their mortality as we watched the great sacrifices of the medical world, ambulance drivers, morticians, even grocery workers. All this painful generosity and yet so many were dying.

I think my generation began to realize the terror and sacrifice of World War II. Mostly we scoffed when our parents bored us with stories. But now that the world was going upside down, not to mention the crazy climate change we were now experiencing, we better understood the hell our parents went through.

Also unavoidable was this country's ancient *racism,* that big word, enveloping everyone not white, whatever white was—maybe the ability to slip into a crowd and avoid the humiliation and fear of being different. But no one was avoiding pain this time around, whatever color or side you were on. We were stripped, nothing was going back to whatever it was—good or bad. Crazy people believed the virus was attached to China. Asian women were knocked down in the streets of New York and San Francisco where they had lived for decades. All kinds of beliefs rattled peoples' brains and created division and fear-mongering stories.

I had been wrestling my way through *Caste* by Isabel Wilkerson. Her examples of racial cruelty were unbearable and true. She stacked them up at the beginning. I took a deep dive in and I knew that if I wanted to read the book all the way to the end, I had to slow down. Ten pages a night, I assigned myself, like doing sit-ups, developing a muscle to bear human cruelty and violence. Not to accept it, but to look at it—to be real, on the ground, to witness what human beings, misguided, are capable of.

I had read her first book years ago when I was laid up in bed with the flu. About the migration of Blacks out of the South, *The Warmth of Other Suns* won the National Book Critics Circle Award for nonfiction. I still had images in my head from that book: the Black medical doctor, tired, driving to California, unable to find a hotel that would take him for a night on the way; the tenant farmer escaping the South out of horror at how a group of white landowners beat a black man.

Many years later, I imagine this dialogue:

> Why you leaving? You're a good worker.
> Leaving 'cause what you did to Willie.
> We'd never do that to you.

He was out of there with his family and I was glad.

Caste was about forming castes, always wanting some-one below you so you could feel better, superior. I finished the book early one evening. At the end, the author used examples from her own life of disrespect and grievous acts committed against her, even when she was traveling first class on a plane for her work. Her examples seared my brain, they felt so close. Because I read it slowly, I could feel the author's brilliant narrative structure, how she built the bones of her story.

On day two in the old cabin from before the First World War, I was facing the need to churn out pages of anti-internet arguments, while at the same time knowing the internet was blooming. I needed something to show for my time, overlooking the big bay, the white ferry with the green top chasing back and forth several times a day to Whidbey Island. I could angle my neck to the left and see the San Juans in the distance, and way to the north-west, conditions clear, I could see Mount Baker with its top sawed off, a volcano not erupting. And way to the east—or south, I wasn't sure—was Mount Rainier, in the Cascade Range, the tallest in the state at 14,410 feet, taller than anything in New Mexico. A whole stretch of volcanoes line Oregon and Washington.

My mind could wander endlessly about the wonders of this place, but I needed to feel pen on paper again, forming language like strung-out ants across white sheets. It's true, I knew very little about internet mechanics, but this I surely knew: my writing students in the last years had become dull, not alive to what's around them. I was aware from the very beginning of teaching in my thirties that students essentially came to class to arouse their passion, a love for seeing, smelling, feeling, looking. They loved when I demanded specificity: forsythia, wild cherry, columbine, cucumber, celery, morning glory, pecans, elms, snails, crickets, butter. Ordinary things that, by naming them, pulled life out of them—or poured life into them. Now, with so many of us in front of computers or cell phones, I needed a sledgehammer to make students alive again to their own life.

Yahoo, I wanted to say. Don't look up anything with your device. Meet the leaves of an oak. As Bashō, the great Japanese haiku writer, said, "If you want to know a tree, go to the tree." I say, if it's salt, pour it in your hand. Taste it. Smell, examine. What does it have to say to you? What do you want to say to it? *Your grandmother didn't put enough on the brisket?* You may go anywhere with common table salt; write in the past, the present, what does salt hold in the future?

I had taught for fifty years, and students, hungry for their own expression, but not having a clue, could be easily directed. I'd make them write and write with their hands on paper till their own pain lifted and their lives spoke through them, clear and specific.

But now as everyone was ensconced in screens and information quickly available, people were unable to even give directions to their own home. Desire to form language, even indications to where you lived, was gone. The pleasure of announcing a left at the big cottonwood on the corner, or a right after Al's Deli, a place you love, was no longer shared. This fine privilege of telling directions was discarded for efficiency. No relishing that the front yard by the setback apartment house was once a bramble of old wild roses not yet in bloom, or a large granite rock split down the middle was a turn for the parking lot.

Sitting on that gnarled couch in the living room, fluffing up the cushion—was this cushion also from the early 1900s?—the other three odd empty bedrooms with naked mattresses surrounding this main room, I picked up the pen and reached way back to my authority. I laughed. I had no authority anymore, but I still had memory, trusting the jagged way time comes back to meet you.

It was the year 2000. I moved to Saint Paul, Minnesota, where I was living for a year and a half, studying Zen koans, ancient stories between students, teachers, friends, a way to sink into the deepest unattached recesses of the mind where I all-at-once existed and didn't exist. The challenges ran up the bones of my spine like piano keys. *What is the sound of one hand clapping?* Tell me, *What is your original face before your parents were born?* Where do I find answers for these questions? Not in my busy brain, but with my whole body; not thinking, but in the luminous moment.

My girlfriend at the time, however, was not with me in Saint Paul. Michele lasted six months in the city of F. Scott Fitzgerald; the Midwest was foreign to her. But even she admitted (she was originally from the Upper East Side of Manhattan) they had good bread shops. It was the wheat capital, after all. But she was not as entranced as I was with this center of the country. She headed west to Palo Alto, where she had worked at Sun Microsystems. Her name as intellectual property lawyer was affixed to the history of the creators of Java, the computer language.

At the end of the year after Michele left the Midwest, I promised I would join her in Palo Alto, where she was in the middle of creating a start-up as the chief operating officer with four engineers, a marketing person, and a CEO.

When I got there, I was shocked by the outright beauty of the California oaks, the rosebushes, the well-kept homes and the busy gardeners blowing grass clippings all over the curb. This was March, but everything was already in bloom. The start-up had established their offices in an old Peninsula dairy and for their first round of funding were seeded by a group of entrepreneurs. They weren't sure what direction their development was going, but everyone was smart, energetic, full of hope, young, agile.

We had been together five days in California when I was going to join Michele at the headquarters to meet the computer engineers. She said they slept late, so introductions would have to begin around two o'clock. "You mean like teenagers?" I asked. They were in their early- to mid-twenties, and yes, I think they had gone to college.

It all felt new out there in the land of dot com. I still had my head in sixth-century CE China, the grit and grain of how to transmit ancient teachings through the whole being of a human so it can be passed down through generations. I knew nothing about computers, had built and lived in a beer can and tire house on a mesa in Taos, New Mexico, off the grid, with car batteries on my roof to collect energy for my solar cells. This technology I had instituted in the mid-Eighties. New Mexico is crazy with sun. My stereo in the house was a car radio and I had an old propane refrigerator run with a tank out back. I was itching to go home to New Mexico after Saint Paul, but I had promised Michele I would join her in California.

Odd that I was with someone like Michele, more urban, hip on current technology. I could feel in the streets of Palo Alto the old orchards, now gone, this once-sleepy little college town now bursting its seams. Alfa Romeos, Corvettes, even a Lamborghini—the fancy cars of my former students' grade school dreams—raced a block and stopped, nowhere to go, revved their engines, too much power for this small municipality with well-cut lawns, perfectly maintained shrubs, overpriced quaint houses—like twenty-dollar handkerchiefs jacked up to $2 million and no one questioning it.

But Michele had many fine qualities. Below her sharp mind and legal agility, she had a broken heart, which meant a soft one. Her people, namely her grandmother and mother, dodged Auschwitz; but relatives she never met—her grandfather, uncle, great-grandparents—did not survive. She was a modern woman with an echo of historical distrust, a ring of sorrow in her bones. We don't know why we are attracted to someone (or, for that matter, attracted to a different religion from the one we are born into; by the time I arrived in Palo Alto, I had many years of Zen meditation under my Jewish belt). But it did seem, even with my present relationship, that I was drawn to people with extreme computer knowledge. In the Seventies, Yu-kwan was one of the few women who worked with men to put Wall Street on computers. I think I was curious and understood that was where a certain present energy lived. But I was still distrustful and lazy. Last summer I hired someone for computer lessons once a week for two months. I took wild notes all over my notebook and as soon as he left, all the instructions left my head and my notes made no sense.

I was aware that to young people it was as natural as it was for me to dial a landline, but my fear was that people lived in those machines, even stated they were addicted. I needed them to have other activities, especially to write about. I'm sure some do, but some need to be led to other wonders. Actually, I know this was true. When I was young, I was glued to the TV. We had three in our house and they were always on. No one stopped me from watching. I had to assert real effort when I left home to discover my own natural interests.

Several people suggested I read *Four Arguments for the Elimination of Television* by Jerry Mander. A handful of good books on the subject of television are out there, and I don't think it's much different from the way internet devices can flatten brain cells.

Upfront, the dairy offices still had an active creamery. The floors were old squares of linoleum, off-white walls—maybe we'd stop for a cone after the meeting? The conference room was empty, save for two tables pushed together and a line of half-opened windows. I remember we sat down in one corner and waited.

In bopped two of the engineers with open-handed hi's. Both in T-shirts, one turquoise, the other orange. The second wore a cap backward on his head. A third strolled in. Half-curious about me, but not really, though friendly. The fourth came at half past. He was getting married in Korea, and the other three planned to fly over and attend.

How long have you known her? Have any of you ever been to Asia? What will you all wear to the ceremony? I asked.

The groom had known his fiancée for a short time. None had been overseas. No answers about their clothes or outfits. They looked at one another and shrugged.

Michele asked if they were coming up with anything new.

The six figures was seed money, I surmised.

A faster Napster product was tried but they could be sued. They changed directions. They were attempting different formats for an enterprise within a company.

"What industry do you think we could do file sharing with—and get acquired?" the latecomer asked. He sat down next to Michele.

Then they loped into a discussion of how revolutionary the internet was. It would save humanity.

I held back from rolling my eyes. Maybe my generation was just as blind with all the LSD we took, stumbling around the woods, thinking we would create a new world order.

I did experience these engineers' brain waves as jagged, disconnected patterns—maybe they were fueled by all those cupcakes with pink icing and the cans of highly caffeinated drinks on the table. But I also felt something else. I had studied the mind firsthand, both in writing and in sitting cross-legged for years, and I felt something odd from these computer programmers. I wondered if the vibration from computers was cutting, lacerating the normal rhythms of the human mind.

Scientists have proven that the brain is malleable, and if not given room to breathe, it can morph and reshape itself, losing innate awake dimensions. Though the internet has the appearance of expansion, it narrows and limits

experience. Instead of being out there swimming or running, talking to another person, bodies are immobile, the
only ride is the machine, no sweat under the arms.

Those programmers in Palo Alto thought their love of
computers was a passion, an opening into life, but instead
it seemed to be a diminishment. That hit of entering the
computer, flicking on the switch, fades everything else but
what's on the screen. The internet encourages skimming,
rarely settling in to read a whole article.

I have to admit I liked email, but I noticed I couldn't
sink into full communication or really be receptive—a
friend writes she has cancer; a town in California burned
down. I keep moving through the line of emails—a thought
to this one, a dash of comment to that one, a fast nod to
another—chop, chop, chop. If I didn't watch it, my mind
would be ground to hamburger meat. I often missed the
real communication in each missive. I didn't create time to
digest them. It reinforced a bland heart, a numb attitude,
and bolstered the feeling of accomplishment—I breezed
through twenty-two emails in record time.

In the middle of the night, I jerked up. "What? My old
friend is dying of cancer?" Anything important moved to
the periphery of my perception and jumped out at me
during rare moments of space. I remember being alone
in a café, picking up a piece of cherry pie with my fork,
remembering an email I read earlier: "She's coming to
visit next week?" I had agreed, then forgotten, leaping to
the next message.

One fine pleasure: punching keys with four fingers of each hand, I feel gratitude to my twelfth grade typing teacher. I can't remember her name or what she looked like and I almost didn't take the class, an elective that seemed useless—like French. I'd never get to go to a foreign country. But here I was, typing away, chug chug chug. Thank you, typing teacher.

Social media, I never touched. It would have scrambled my instincts for good. So I can't speak to the hate and violence it let loose. It scared me. Young bright kids, one in particular, had a good idea in his sophomore year at Harvard; but he was a kid, not the appropriate person to run an internet company that grew to such influence and finance, capable of destroying lives with what people wrote about each other. The internet was becoming unhinged, way beyond one good idea.

Point One: Stop looking at it all the time.

My assistant teacher, back before Covid, said, "The important thing is, you give students alternative things to do."

There is going for a walk without a device.

There is looking at an actual map and going for a ride, getting lost and finding your way home without using a device. How? Drive up and down streets, wander.

I hope there is still making love without using a device for instructions.

Ride a bike sans a device.

In Sweden everyone must have a full month vacation, and it is illegal during that time for them to be contacted via a device.

See if there is a farm near you or someone growing food. Buy some fresh produce. Watch the corn grow.

Okay, Point Two: Read a book.

A real book, cover to cover. Sure, it can be an ebook, but you are missing the weight in your hands, the weird marker you can pick to delineate what page you left off on yesterday. Make sure to pick a book you really like, so you'll hang with it and finish. Go to a library, peruse a bookstore. What is your lilt of mind? See if you can find a book not published in the last five years that has some staying power and value. Who is it dedicated to? The publishing date can be found on the copyright page, usually on the other side of the title page, in the front. (I'm not being condescending. Most of my students paid no heed to these details.)

The phone rang. It was Eddie. We had a planned call.

"Hey, how are you? Leg healed?" I asked first thing.

"My PT said to be patient."

"Are you going crazy?" I knew he wasn't. I'm always trying to poke into the dark side of his nature, but it doesn't work.

"I heard Mary say on the phone to someone that I was a good patient." A pause. "I have to be. This is a long haul."

"You are so smart. I'd be enraged and alienate everyone. Yu-kwan by this time would have left me. I'd be alone, screaming, in the living room."

"How's your memory?" He was referring to our word practice.

"Going fast." Then I told him what I was writing about.

He was thinking, I could tell. "I sent you a book. I just read it. It's a lot of what we've talked about—from another angle. White men in charge and how fatal that can be."

Eddie had never sent me a book before. "Thank you. I'll keep a lookout for it. I'll check the Centrum office."

"It's not bad to write about something you don't know about. It gives a fresh outlook," he added. We both laugh. "But I'm serious," he said. I'd told him I was writing about computers and what they do to human beings.

"I need that encouragement," I said.

We scheduled a call for the next week.

An addition to Point Two: Don't use your device to look for a book to read. Find it on your own. Wander the library, bookstores, book reviews, newspapers, and magazines. Also, ask a friend what book they love.

Each day I kept writing, like I promised at Hemingway's grave, but I could feel all the confidence draining out of me, afraid anything I said would be laughed at. I was back to being a beginning writer, how I felt thirty-five years ago when I sat at that electric Smith Corona, typing out my first book. Like many others during this bizarre pandemic time, I had lost direction, my true north. But I saw now that the world wasn't going to get better. Everything would be different. I couldn't wait around. I hoped that if I kept advancing the pen, that the critical voice would shut up, not have so much authority. I was groundless, pretending, and kept my hand moving.

In the middle of my pull, yank, and tug, I drove not far to downtown Port Townsend: small, population ten thousand. I had heard it was a place where old hippies came to die. On Water Street was Imprint Books, a store of new volumes, and across the street was William James, a huge used bookstore. They sent people back and forth to find what they wanted. I perused Imprint, checking if they were selling my latest, *Three Simple Lines.* I found a single slim volume.

As I pushed open the door to leave, I backtracked. *Dirt* by Bill Buford came to mind. Only in hardback. I'd heard it was out. Lately I had read a lot of books by women and people of color—and rarely taught anything else—but I adored Buford's *Heat* when I read it at least fifteen years ago. He was a *New Yorker* editor who dropped out and moved to Italy to learn Italian cooking. I savored the pleasure of it for years and recommended it.

This time, he traveled with his twin sons and wife to France to learn French cooking. Unlike the US, where a person can get a paid restaurant job with little experience, in France, even if you go to cooking school, you have to apprentice for free for at least a year. You find a restaurant where you want to learn, apply, and hope they will take you.

I went back to the cashier at the bookstore and ordered *Dirt.* Buford's very first book, *Among the Thugs,* documented the seduction of crowd violence at football/soccer games in the United Kingdom and was popular. *Dirt* was buried at publication because of Covid. (And maybe also because white men were defunct during this epidemic time.) I hadn't seen it in any stores.

When the hefty hardback with the bright red cover arrived, I brought this almost secret pleasure, this 432-page book, back to my solo living quarters, which felt like a hidden den, deep and far away. Behind the cottages was the fort of rusted bunkers, designed before World War I to protect Seattle from enemy ships or tankers moving into the bay. Not one shot was ever fired in defense, and no enemies came this way. However, it was good cover for me to read a white male writer. No one would see me. I felt protected.

That very night I opened *Dirt* and began. It wasn't easy for Buford's family of four, the twins at two years old, the wife who thankfully spoke French, to pull up New York roots, ship their belongings, and arrive in a foreign country. The parents knew that their kids, always with linguistic flex, on the edge of learning English, could also quickly pick up their new language. Poor Bill, the author, had only his clunky original tongue, not the native one of the new country, and was the one who had to maneuver in foreign kitchens.

I sank into the book after a week of residency, keeping bright lights on in the bedroom even though the light outside was late fading. An electric radiator along the bottom wall of the bedroom rattled, and the single narrow window, the only operative one, was open wide, but gave little air. Wearing a cheap white nightgown purchased years ago from Target, I derived right from the beginning a pleasure only a good book with good writing can give you. After much back and forth, the family settled in Lyon, not a romantic town, but everyone advised, if you want real cuisine, this town is the heart of French cooking.

Reading took me inside another country: the smell of baking wafting into the sounds of cars rattling on uneven pavement, leading up to the terrible machinations of trying, especially as an American, to place yourself as an apprentice in a renowned chef's kitchen, to be okayed for a payless menial job, proving yourself enough to finally work up to peeling onions, maybe even cutting them. But I must admit I garnered delight in the miserable way the younger staff of more experienced men treated him, pitilessly testing his resolve, Buford being the lowest, the most vulnerable. I'm not a cruel person, but this was so much fun. It was pointed out to him that he was too slow cutting peppers because he crossed his hands. "You must never cross them." Peppers on left, knife on right, tray for finished peppers in center.

And of course, he had writing credentials, so the kitchen crew in reverse snobbery really turned the screws. An effete writer? Who cares. This is physical work, man's work.

A bit of the way into the book a French woman dared to appear as an apprentice. She was courageous, wanting to earn her living eventually in the food industry, but first enduring the awful apprenticeship. The work crew made her life miserable with vile gestures at her back as she peeled and cut carrots. Buford sympathized, being in a similar position. I sympathized, too, and was rooting for her. They were a tough bunch, these male cooks.

Days later, I was in the middle, the meat of the book, wishing instead of 432 pages that the book was 1,500 pages. I wanted it never to end. Every cell, every extremity— toes, fingers, nose, top of my head—was absorbed in this crappy kitchen behavior all the way over in Lyon, France, a town I had never been to.

All I knew how to do in French was conjugate the verb *être,* to be. Six years of French in middle school and high school, two in college. I was a language dummy and my pronunciation was appalling, like a Brooklyn person with marbles in her mouth. But I could order a mean hot fudge sundae *avec* whipped cream—that I did learn on the spot in a Paris café.

Henry Miller, the great and productive American writer, mistakenly believing in the romance of France, spent time in Lyon. After a short interval he complained while sitting on a bench at the Lyon station, eager to leave, that all the town did was belch out the smell of mustard.

I had my own sobering experience of small-town France a few years ago reading *The End of Eddy,* a memoir of a young gay boy's childhood in small-town France. I imagined every French home full of elegance, a thin-throated pale vase on the table, a slightly drooping daffodil or a bunch of grape hyacinths, a kitchen window slightly ajar, lace curtains fluttering, always an open attitude toward sex, maybe even a raunchy display in the bedroom. Not so, in this case: the Eddy of this book suffered with strict, narrow-minded parents, the father a hired hand, and a heavy hand on his son. It was more an image I had of small-town USA. France was changed for me with this memoir, full of anti-Semitic slurs.

But with Buford, I was ricocheted back to a writer who could handle and write about Lyon's culinary scrappy kitchens, years after Miller's sojourn and Eddy's small-town suffering. Even with recommendations, Buford had trouble finding work. So he first apprenticed with Bob, the baker, next door to the family's apartment. As I read, I could smell the long baguettes, still hot; the feel of leaning into the mass of dough at 3 A.M.; the sound of the crust cracking as one of his young sons breaks off the end and stuffs the bread into his mouth when he stops in right before school.

I used the book to seduce myself into the back ill-ventilated bedroom at night. Even though I left that window open all the time, little air moved. And this was the best of the four bedrooms. I wouldn't allow reading during the day. I had to create discipline. Instead, I pushed myself into the internet manuscript I half-heartedly believed someone might be interested in, but also knew it was important. As I went deeper into my own simple pleasure of reading, young minds were drowning in their screens.

It's the fifth day of class, and I ask students an impossible question: "Who can tell what I found interesting the first morning when we went around, and I asked what you fear?"

A great silence ensues; then they begin popping out answers.

"Stop. You are grabbing for things. Don't reach. Let the answer rise from the bottom of your mind." I add, "Like dead fish coming up from the bottom of the lake."

The class drops. You can feel it. They are settling. Also damn curious.

The woman in the back with a red tattoo on her arm says something.

"Close, but not it."

How would they know what I was thinking? What this question does is make them receptive, creates a space in their minds, some curiosity. When I drop in the answer, a sigh, an *ahh*. Room to receive it.

Point Three: When we quickly look up answers on the internet, information becomes a commodity; we grab and forget. It allows no dwelling in the unknown. It allows no mystery. Don't bypass the odd way memory moves and the way we digest experience. When will you die, where and how? Your computer can't tell you that.

The sun sets late in Port Townsend, way up near Canada. I was creeping to the back bedroom earlier and earlier. I'm pretty sure it was a Wednesday night—the garbage was collected every other midweek day and that morning I'd put mine out—I was so engrossed, eyes tearing, head bent, body a curve over the text, that I must have felt gone, not solid but sparkling like a sprinkler twirling around on the green lawn of my childhood. I laughed so hard at one point in the book, the kind of laughter that carried me back to the intense youth of fourth grade concentration, when I sat at the edge of my Long Island bed reading a Freddy the Pig book by Walter R. Brooks. It's hard to find that series now. Another life, nine years old, not mine anymore, like ice broken off a glacier, gone forever. But that night my laughter felt so intense it broke open my whole imagined timeline; past, present, future merged. I was even the great Buddha that night, not peaceful, but in a frenzy of broken beliefs. I collapsed at 3 A.M. in happy exhaustion.

Laughter, happiness, a fresh start was badly needed during the pandemic. Do not underrate glee in hard times. Captured by Nazis, Jews drew cartoons of their predicament—it kept their own independent angle on their suffering.

I rolled out of bed the next day at one in the afternoon,

sun high in the sky—it's not always that sunny out here in the Pacific Northwest. I stretched and yawned, imagining Mount Rainier, a true empress, could be seen if I went down to the beach. I took a long shower, a pleasure of the Pacific Northwest. They seemed to have endless water. (That will change along with the climate catastrophe.) In New Mexico I saved all gray water for the compost; otherwise, without moisture, the compost wouldn't decompose.

Feeling clean, I walked up behind the cabin to the top of Fort Worden and stood for some time reading the poems by Sam Hamill, inscribed in bronze on tall thin columns, a memorial installation and sculpture garden known as Memory's Vault. It was a curious memorial, honoring the old life of the fort, with the corroded bunkers dug deep into the earth, rimming the bluff. Now a state park, the fort was originally built in the late-nineteenth and early-twentieth centuries, protecting Puget Sound. These parts of Hamill's poems went right to the core:

THE BUNKERS

A foolish man might say it's in our blood, that long recorded history of our need to fortify, to train our guns on anything that moves or breathes.

The birds don't understand. Teals scud slowly down the Strait. Gulls cry out for gulls. Quail in the underbrush and the gentle song of a mourning dove.

BLACK MARSH ECLOGUE

Although it is midsummer, the great blue heron
holds darkest winter in his hunched shoulders,
those blue-turning-gray clouds
rising over him like a storm from the Pacific.

He stands in the black marsh
more monument than bird, a wizened prophet
returned from a vanished mythology.
He watches the hearts of things

and does not move or speak. But when
at last he flies, his great wings
cover the darkening sky, and slowly,
as though praying, he lifts, almost motionless

as he pushes the world away.

Hamill had translated Bashō's *Journey to the Deep North* for Shambhala Publishing but his title was *Narrow Road to the Interior.* That's how I heard of him, but when I read his bio—living on the streets during the Beat heyday of the Fifties, began a Zen Buddhist practice in Okinawa and was a conscientious objector, founding editor of Copper Canyon Press, a renowned poetry publisher—I felt foolish that I had declined a chance to meet him two years before. Each reading of his poems—I'd gone up there many times—deepened my understanding of this northern land, not unlike the landscapes of Japan, where I'd been several times, searching for Zen and haiku roots. With hands dug deep into my pants' pockets, I was sorry again I missed my chance to meet this human being and honor him. On this second time I'd come to the Centrum Residency, I was told he had died.

I climbed down from the top of Fort Worden, still in a bit of a daze from waking at one in the afternoon, and drove to the Port Townsend Food Co-op. It was autumn; there were twenty-six kinds of apples—I counted them— and eight different pears. A lot of fresh-caught fish, abundant vegetables. I imagined it was a lot like California in the Sixties when "organic" was discovered; small fertile farms served affordable produce before California became fancy. Here were the bakeries with flour from grain grown a mile away, robust fresh eggs. *Shh.* It's a secret I fell upon by the extraordinary luck of being a resident writer at Centrum.

Or maybe it wasn't luck. Often, I bemoaned my need to write, like an endless term paper, still at my desk, still doing my assignment, wondering if my tough, wonderful high school English teacher Mr. Cates would approve of what I wrote. But oh, how miserable I was these last two years during the pandemic when no writing came. A writer's block? Hogwash. I don't believe in that. Well, maybe a little. I doubted, did not trust I had anything useful to say. My voice came out as an insecure croak, but the malaise was deeper. I questioned the whole ground: Shouldn't I shut up and make way for writing by people of color? What use do I have? The world is moving on with those machines (computers in all forms), and I've pretty much dropped out of the whole fast vast net that people seemed to believe in—I didn't drink the Kool-Aid this time. But it was also Covid. We were all stunned into silence.

Yet I still had Point Four: Please don't call me to tell me you are late. I know you are late because you are not here.

What is ten minutes? Fifteen? Those devices build insecurity. We have a date: Come. Don't worry. Just show up.

I call Eddie. I want to tell him about the glories of *Dirt,* but first I ask, "Eddie, how are you doing?"

"I've gotten good at maneuvering the wheelchair. I don't need help. The PT person said to give it another month and I can try standing on my leg."

"How about doing a topic, you know, like in writing practice, but do it orally. Ten minutes each," I suggest.

"Ten minutes. I never talk for that long. No."

"C'mon. You can have spaces of silence that count in the ten minutes, and next time we talk you can come up with the topic, your choice," I cajole him.

"Okay, what's the topic?"

"What will you miss when you die."

Long silence on the other end of the phone. Then, "I hope this time is counting."

"Yes." I roll my eyes. I imagine him looking around for things he'll miss, but he's a good sport.

"Birds. I'll miss birds." A pause. "Mary, of course. My sons, even though I don't see one of them enough. My dog." Jetta is the loudest barking dog in America—and when he calms down, when he sees you're a friend, you could probably steal the whole house and he wouldn't mind. "I'm getting tired."

"You only have two more minutes."

"Writing, my desk. New Mexico. Biking—when I get better. Sex. Touch. Are the two minutes up?"

"Thirty more seconds.

"I won't miss you when I die," he spurts out. We both burst out laughing. "Why don't you write me yours. I have to nap."

We say goodbye. I'm sad. I hope he is okay.

I return to the cottage. I plop on the couch. I pop up. Cut off a hunk of cheese I bought at the co-op. I never eat dairy, but I was alone. In my secret life I can eat what I want. In my secret life my body never complains. I kick off my shoes. I pick at a candle that dripped days ago. I write a card to a friend. It is already getting dark. The day moves fast since I woke up late. I was so happy—and now I am anxious—will I fall asleep tonight? Sleep is not easy this month. I have to be patient, lie still in bed for hours before sleep comes.

I sit down, take out my notebook, and write to tell Eddie what I'll miss when I die, using writing practice, keeping

my hand moving, which means losing control and not necessarily sticking to the topic, but rather following my mind.
I begin:

> *I'll miss a lilac bush in spring, thinking of my mother,*
> *bored as a housewife, bored with her two children,*
> *the blood of fear coursing in her, unknowingly, even*
> *before World War II, transmitted from her parents,*
> *escaping pogroms, but stopping in front of a fragrant*
> *bush, everything dropped away. She put her nose in the*
> *pale purple, then white, tall lilacs along Oak Neck Lane*
> *and declared with a smile, "These are my favorites." I*
> *can envision the lumpy tarred country road, the Dairy*
> *Queen at the end, Atlantic Ocean at the other end, in*
> *shadows of elm, early May of my youth when Uncle*
> *Sam had Twin Oaks, a broken-down estate in Bay Shore*
> *on Long Island. It is the one time my mother conveyed*
> *pure pleasure. (Please, Mothers, tell your daughters what*
> *you love for beauty or pleasure's sake, that they may*
> *wake to the season before summer or the season after*
> *summer and hold the memory of you in happiness, long*
> *after you have passed.)*

I later lie in bed, thinking I should drop this internet
manuscript. No one could ever get people to ditch their
TVs. The internet is the new thing—everyone wants the
new thing. We all want to belong, be connected. But
twenty-four hours a day?

I jump out of bed—I can't help it—Point Five: Go for a walk. At least be outside for an hour. No device. Sit on a bench if you want and have a little rest. Look around. Faded cigarette ad on the brick wall of a building; cracks in the sidewalk; a city bus pulls up. How many things can you see? Maybe bring a little notebook and list twenty ordinary objects.

A tree counts. Can you name what kind of tree?

The next morning, I finger *Dirt*. I have so few pages left. It comes to me, the title, what it means: the dirt, the real truth, the underbelly of training for French cooking. The misery, especially if a woman tries to break through. In the whole book I learned one helpful cooking hint: instead of cracking a raw egg on the edge of a bowl (often, with too much energy I accidentally smash the whole shell), tap it lightly on a flat surface. Then separate the shell with your fingers over the cooking pan. That was told as a simple declarative reminder to Buford. I wasn't reading the book to learn about cooking anyway. Most of the enjoyment was between people, told through close detail. The reader could easily picture it. Also, the torture in the back kitchen, abuse and macho challenge. Oh, and how I loved it. What was wrong with me? None of my friends had any interest.

Michel Richard, who back in the United States inspired Buford to make Lyon and its kitchens his home, flew to meet Buford in France after many months. Richard now had many eateries in the United States, fed people on trains and airplanes, and owned a great pastry shop in Los Angeles, but he wanted to take Buford back to his past, to the original pâtisserie where he began training in Lyon.

Léon, eighteen years old, was the chef. "He liked to hit me. You make a mistake, you get smacked. 'You burned your croissants!' Smack. 'You didn't clean this corner!' Smack. 'You cooked a meringue in a copper pot!' Smack. 'You ground the almonds too fast and the rollers are stuck! *Imbecile! Putain de merde!* You don't make mistakes!'" Education by humiliation.

"I was at my station, my back to the kitchen, and a knife flew by my head and pierced the wall in front of me. The chef thought it was funny."

Richard hit him on the head with a rolling pin and knocked him unconscious. Finally, the two had established a rapport.

"For three years, I never went home. I never saw a movie. I learned everything: *apprendre, apprendre, apprendre.*"

On September 3, 1965, Richard took his pâtisserie proficiency exams. The French system: You do an apprenticeship, you take an exam, and you are certified. He was now a trained chef.

"Monsieur Sauvage never did any work, except at Christmas when we started at four a.m. and worked until ten at night. But Monsieur (Léon) Sauvage loved me. He never said so. But I could tell."

After Richard left, he phoned Monsieur Sauvage every year just before the new year, thanking him for taking him on. "He gave me something."

I finished the last sweet pages of Buford's journey. How I laughed the night before, like bright bubbles I used to blow as a kid. Such pleasure.

One day later I receive a book in the mail from Eddie with a note: "You have to read this." Hardback. A lot smaller than *Dirt*. I sniff around it, read the back cover, the insert, examine the title page. I don't want to read this: First, it appears to be about science; second, I don't want to read anything but what I just read. I feel like an empty lot with some old beer cans, a few plastic straws, even an old diaper in the corner—it's how devoid and lost I feel after finishing a really good book. What's going to fill my mind now? I don't want to move on. There can't be anything else, like after winning a big race or the last bite of an apple pie you made. Nothing left. Reading is like this. Reading is a sport. Only, the muscle is hidden, not overt.

Basically, I don't want to read *Why Fish Don't Exist* by Lulu Miller. Nothing personal, I'm just spent. But this is the first book Eddie has ever sent me. I feel obligated to read it, but I feel a bit of betrayal to Buford whom I bonded with, who worked so hard. It's not even *just* science, it's about biology. Doesn't Eddie know?

I begin the new book. I cannot put it down—I now sound like a reading hussy, one after the other. But this new book is good.

At the same time, I am grunting through this internet manuscript. I still had my landline, but because I wasn't home, I now had a cell phone. When I spoke on it, I held it far away, certain it would give me ear or cheek cancer.

Point Six: You don't have to know everything. If I say, "I wonder who was on the Yankees last year before they left New York for Los Angeles," I'm just *wondering.* Give me a break and some space to wonder, daydream, and most of all, *to not know.*

A whole immense life is out there, untouchable by a computer, unknowable by a computer. Go out and live it.

I have a sacred winter hike. It's difficult and in the middle are no markers on how to get up the ridge. Each time you have to find your way. Only two other people even know about it: my Taos friend who took me one New Year's Day years ago and her husband who came along. It is a tradition when you arrive on the rambling top where you can see the Rio Grande and even way in the distance Taos Mountain, you light a joint. You don't even have to toke it. Sometimes I have ingested the smoke which makes the meandering way down even harder. Every year I hike it, and if I am lucky, on the way down I wander into the elk meadow where a herd sleeps at night. I can see in the long, deep winter grass shapes indented from the night before. A trickling stream is on the edge of the meadow and under thin ice water-cress is still green and alive.

Three years ago, I took a good friend from California. I appreciated her willingness to join me. The altitude was high and her lungs weren't accustomed. We had a won-derful time but when we got back to the car she read on her wrist: *six miles.* My body slunk behind the driver's wheel. The mileage never occurred to me. It was simply: the sacred winter hike. (In all fairness it was my friend's daughter who gave her the watch that tells all. My friend was trying to stay *au courant* with the next generation for her children's sake.)

Point Seven: Please don't commodify everything. Whether we put our mind and heart in a box, or put all our surroundings into a box. The same thing. No miles. Distance out there as far as the eye can see.

All things end. Another writer needs my cabin. My month is up. I do not want to leave. I crazily contact a real estate agent. I will buy a place. It's 2020, people are scrambling out of cities, working at home with Zoom. There is no inven-tory in Port Townsend. Not a single place. My fingernails dig into the dirty white siding of the cabin. *No, I can't go.*

My partner has flown back. We plan to drive to the

Olympic Peninsula, to the Hoh Rainforest. The real estate agent promises to contact me if a small house goes up for sale.

"Let's go back," I say. We are four miles out of town. "I need one last croissant." I swing the car into a U. My partner complies. It is the best croissant in America. I get a chocolate; she, a ham and cheese. I eat as I drive, turning west. Not talking much. I take the last bite.

PART IV

ELK

AFTER MY GREAT month in Port Townsend, Yu-kwan and I meandered home. We headed west to the Hoh part of the Olympic National Forest, the only temperate rainforest in North America. *Hoh* is clearly from a Native American language, but I could find no clarity of its origin or translation; the stab at it I liked best was "man with quarreling wives." Rain fell almost all the time, and even when rain wasn't falling, everything was so wet. A lush, thick canopy created a dark green aura even at noon, and dense mosses and ferns blanketed the ground. The Hoh is magical, but it also made me a bit nervous. Where is the light? The oxygen was thick, and my lungs loved it, but not forever. I could imagine lichen growing in the two bags of my lungs. I could also imagine in this weather, wives quarreling.

On the first late afternoon as dim sunlight stole small moments through the lush overhead of big-leaf maples,

Sitka spruces, and Douglas firs, off a narrow road a herd of Roosevelt elk, heads down, were feeding on the tall grass. We stopped and gaped. After my father died twenty years ago, I dreamed he became an elk in a herd and we no longer had the same language. I'd never seen elk so close or anything so beautiful as these animals, especially the females. I wanted to be an elk just then with all my heart. A long time passed, and they moved on. We had to move on, too, though I didn't want to.

The next day I ached to see them again, like a hunger for home. Yu-kwan commiserated. We returned to where we saw them. A long shot, but we lingered in the grass. I pulled up a blade and chewed on the edge. Yu-kwan nudged me on the arm, pointed with her chin. A branch moved and one male with two huge females stepped out of the dense forest. Immediately, they lowered their heads. We were so near we could hear a long ripping sound as they tore the grass, and then thumps of their jaws as they masticated. I wanted to put my arms around the nearest female with her deep brown hide. No shame in being huge. How I wanted to be full like them and run off on all fours outside of human thought and culture.

I call Eddie when we get to Portland, Oregon. He is doing a lot better. Looking out the hotel window, I report: "It's full of people living on the streets. Yesterday we walked past bedding, hands out for money or food. I feel bad I can't give something, but I'm still afraid of Covid. When I get home, I'll get my first vaccination."

Eddie replies, "Got it last week. Mary had a reaction. All fine now. Maybe you're taking a chance, traveling without it?"

"Yeah, the whole trip is a chance. I've been double masking. Can hardly breathe. Covid is still rampant." I tell him about the Roosevelt elk.

"You have that chronic cancer. Hope it's all okay."

Ah, yes, my chronic cancer. I almost forget about it, the drug I take daily is so good. But I know that someday the cancer, like a cockroach in New York City that eventually turned on its poison and began eating it as food, will find a way around the drug. Since eight years ago when I started to take it, even better solutions have been developed, but my oncologist, Dulcinea (do you believe she has that perfect name?), repeats, "If it's not broken, don't fix it." So I go by faith and try to practice not getting anxious about the whole thing.

"Eddie, I've been hearing from Grove." Grove is a mutual friend, a big environmental lawyer; he used to ride on horseback up over the hill to Eddie's back door. "He's having a hard time. He sends me quotes: 'Do not waste time.' That's from Michelangelo. I quoted that to students in my early teaching from *The Writing Life* by Annie Dillard. I don't know where Grove found it. It means something altogether different now. Hold on. I'll read you what he wrote," I say, and go get my computer to read the whole email to Eddie:

"I'll be fucking 75 in June. Philip Roth had, as I know you know, numerous ailments and physical problems his entire life. He said: 'Aging is not a battle, it is a fucking catastrophe.'

"I burst out laughing when I read that," I tell Eddie. I can feel his pleasure even on the phone.

I continue reading, "Then he says, 'Our dear friend Tolstoy wrote'—Grove and I took an *Anna Karenina* seminar together years ago at St. John's back in Santa Fe—'the biggest surprise in a man's life is BEING'—he's typed it in caps—'fucking old.'"

I wrote Grove back, "I bet Tolstoy didn't include 'fucking' in the quote."

Grove wrote me again—"It's the hardest thing in my life to deal with. I'm lost." He had brought the wolves back to New Mexico. With his wife, Linda, and two other financial supporters, he purchased an inholding in the Carson National Forest, where the powerful Vallecitos River ran through, with beaver ponds, aspens, elk, tallgrass. They created a retreat center.

The Vallecitos Mountain Refuge was a big and idealistic effort. Everything went into creating it. Grove left his lucrative law firm where he'd trained young environmental lawyers. He and Linda moved their family from Santa Fe to Taos to be closer to the refuge. Maya and Cisco, their young kids, started attending a new school.

They built new cabins, redid the old log cabin as a zendo with a grand stone fireplace, and brought in people from all over the country. World-renowned meditation teachers and local teachers taught there. Grove gave everything.

Grove and I took inner-city residents for meditation and writing retreats twelve miles into the forest on a dirt road. At first, I couldn't get them off the porch because they were so scared of the wilderness.

I shake my head in the hotel room, "I wrote to Grove that in a year or two, Bob Dylan will be eighty."

Grove writes back: "It brought tears to my eyes."

Later that day, Yu-kwan and I walk through the front doors of the Portland Art Museum. Several galleries have an exhibition of photos and explanations of the Mount St. Helens volcanic eruption. Whole forests burned, as if the enormous trees were toothpicks covered with lava. Watercolors of the eruption painted by Ursula Le Guin, who lived in Portland, are on the walls. She and a friend drove out to see it. Photos of her with the friend standing in amazement with mouths open are also part of the exhibit. I had not realized from where I lived so many states away how extensive this eruption was. I was catching up now, moving slowly from gallery to gallery.

Another gallery holds Japanese pottery in glass cases. Fukami Sueharu, born 1947, a year before me. The exhibit says he is the most famous living potter. His seascape is a flat blue, modern.

Shingu Sayaka, young, born 1979, has a flair in her pot, an acknowledgment that she's taking the tradition and moving it slightly over, a freedom.

Morino Taimei lives in Japan and threw a traditional pot, slightly off-center, showing its humanness, quietly. Maybe my favorite.

This looking, having time, I do not take lightly. This act of slowing down, these bowls, these vessels, hold time.

As we step outside the Portland Art Museum at the end of the afternoon, my mind feels expansive. I picture my mother's eighty-ninth birthday. It seems so long ago. I flew in the day before. Soon after I arrived, we zipped over to the local Jewish deli.

A young waitress approached our table and I ask, pointing at my mother, "How old do you think my mother is? Tomorrow is her birthday."

The waitress takes a long moment. "Fifty-one?"

My mother and I laugh. Then I realize she is not kidding. "How old are you?" I ask.

"Sixteen."

I try to imagine how old fifty-one must seem when you are sixteen.

My mother looks at the menu. "What are you ordering?" she asks. Then she leans in: "Well, what's it like?" I had returned recently from two weeks in Paris.

"Nice, it was nice. A big city," I say, returning to my old mute self around her.

She asks again. "But what's it like? Do they have shopping centers?" She points out the window. "Like here?"

"Mostly small markets, food stands, book vendors along the Seine, lots of bakeries," I try to explain.

"But do they have department stores? Tell me. Discounts? Sales?"

Our sandwiches are served, but she doesn't stop. "Where do you shop? Do they have big supermarkets? Like Kmart? Walmart? Tell me," she says and cocks her head. I realize she's trying to picture where I've been.

Just then, a big man plops a dish of two rugelach in front of me. He turns to walk away, but my mother grabs his elbow with such force he almost flips over.

"Dessert, what do you have?" she demands.

He looks at her. "I thought you got à la carte?"

"Give her dessert," I implore.

"I'll have the ice cream," she says with huge satisfaction. Then she says to me, "I'll probably never get to France." A moment of silence.

I feel sad. My heart squeezes tight.

PART V

QUEER

TIME FEELS LIKE Vaseline. I have a feeling this virus will follow me to my grave. Not the exact element that will kill me, but will be around, disrupting things, even though people at some point will be free to not wear masks. Mask wearing is natural for me after visiting Japan several times before the pandemic, where masks are customary. Even when I hike now, I wear a mask to protect me from pollen and allergies.

We were naive to think *boom, bam, done with that*. First of all, the virus will keep morphing. Just like us, it wants to stay alive. The 1918 flu had long-term effects; many people endured long convalescences, full of nervous complications, apathy, depression, tremors, sleeplessness. Let us not forget the respiratory tract, how our lungs can be affected. The aftereffects of the 1918 flu sound familiar to what we now call Long Covid. Similar problems followed the other pandemic in 1889, which also broke people financially. They were not able to work and were left pallid, fatigued, and fearful.

After the first two or two-and-a-half years we knew the world would not be the same. Zoom would never have wriggled its way into so many lives if not for the isolation and hunger to be connected. A help wanted sign at a gas station offered $17/hour plus health benefits. The sign was up for a long time. Even with justly increased pay, no one applied. Restaurants closed; others reduced hours because they couldn't find workers.

This different landscape continues. I spend a lot of time alone, dodging gatherings, readings, even no longer going to cafés regularly to hang out and write. I often take long walks down my dirt road with no sidewalks. I have to watch for fast cars. After one mile, I make a sudden left and disappear up a hidden trail. All kinds of images from my past come to mind when I walk, partially because I have so much more space and am not working regularly.

I recall a workshop I held on Madeline Island a few years back. First we caught the ferry in a small town, a village really, at the northern tip of Wisconsin, where they had a good coffee shop and two remarkable bookstores. I found a thin copy of the novel *Winter in the Blood* by James Welch, originally from the Blackfeet culture, at Honest Dog Books. Who could resist that title and a knockout introduction by Louise Erdrich? I had just assigned Erdrich's most recent book, *The Night Watchman,* which won the Pulitzer, to my writing students. Erdrich wrote that she read *Winter in the Blood* over and over before she became a writer. It gave her permission that the lives that she and Welch lived could provide meaningful literature.

The ferry left us at La Pointe, the most western tip on the largest of the Apostle Islands sacred to the Anishinaabe people. Erdrich belongs to this tribe.

I also had assigned *Negroland* by Margo Jefferson and, in an inspired leap, *A Moveable Feast,* thinking the crew who had signed up with me and traveled so far would be delighted to read a classic.

The Wednesday afternoon we were to go over the Hemingway book, my two trusty longtime assistants, Dorotea and Carrie, set up four chairs in the front of the room and chose four of the sixty waving hands of students in attendance. We were creating a panel to comment on the Hemingway book they had read. Each participant had three minutes, and Carrie and Dorotea fed them easy questions to help them, such as, How did you like the book? We planned to do three rounds of four participants, which made twelve in all with comments. I sat on the side to listen and observe.

The first participant stood up: "I hate the book. Who does he think he is? C'mon. He knew Picasso? Who is he kidding? And he spent all his time in French cafés? Give me a break." My mouth fell open. I tried to be objective. My jaw became awfully tight.

It continued like this. One response I particularly remember: "And he puts in French words. I don't speak

French. How did he expect me to know *inaccrochable, framboise, eau-de-vie*," she read from the book with faulty expression. The French words could easily have been figured out from context.

Of course you don't know French, I thought. We are ignorant Americans. We only learn English and think everyone should speak our language.

I also thought: this is the result of the internet. They don't have a historical sense that Picasso and Hemingway were both struggling artists in the Thirties in Paris. They think everything happens in present tense. I also thought: I can't possibly spread the love of the written word across the country. I've been trying for fifty years. I give up. Let the internet win. I'm thankfully on my way out before too much more damage is done.

After the third proud panel round sat down—they'd certainly expressed themselves, no holds barred—I asked, "Now would you like to hear how I feel about the book?"

All heads nodded.

"You know *Writing Down the Bones*"—they all had read it, it's why they were here—"the chapter on writing in cafés?" They all eagerly nodded. "Where do you think I got the idea?" I held *A Moveable Feast* high.

"As a young writer I pored over the pages to get hints on how to write. From his descriptions—the rain in Paris, the snow—I learned to include weather."

I read out loud parts I loved. They cowered. "Please read this book again."

I asked how many had seen the recent three-part documentary. A smattering of hands, few had. "Yes, it's true he didn't live an exemplary life," I told them. "But still he kept showing up to write.

"That's why I teach writing practice. It's my hope to close the gap between someone's fine, deep, connected writing and how they live their life. A writer doesn't have to be mad or an alcoholic to squeeze out their writing. Writing and life can be more coincident, can be seen as a practice. Not holy, not precious. Instead, you show up and continue as long as you live."

In all fairness, three months later, one of the participants wrote me: *I'm learning French.* And another: *I'm saving up to go to Europe. I've never been or conceived before I could do it.*

Sweet.

I continue walking, past stones sparkling with mica and hoofprints of deer, some elk prints, the hooves larger and heavy in the earth. As I reach near the summit, walking through a flat place right before it climbs again, I wonder what those students would have thought of *The Ballad of the Sad Café* by Carson McCullers. We read it in ninth grade in Mr. Cates's class. A novella of seventy pages. I often felt I became a writer because of that book. Miss Amelia, Marvin Macy, Cousin Lymon. I could still recite the main characters' names.

I couldn't remember—wait a minute—maybe this physical exertion, this climbing, knocked the memory loose. We talked in class about the lover and the beloved. How could six-foot-three Miss Amelia love and long for that five-foot-three hunchback Cousin Lymon, who wasn't a "cousin" at all and betrayed her? And then corrupt Marvin Macy gets out of prison, and we find out he once was married to Miss Amelia for a very short time, not much more than a few days. He longed for her and she hated, detested him. Then after prison he wanted to get back at her and there was a hint that Cousin Lymon was enchanted by this freshly freed convict. Was that discussion what made me so enchanted with the book? I doubted it.

What was it anyway about the lover and the beloved? A hidden intuition that McCullers was queer—only revealed long after she was dead? Or that thirty years later, the night I finished typing *Bones* on my Smith Corona after seven weeks of full concentration from the depths of my being, I would flash, *I want to be with a woman now.* That something way back then in ninth grade, in the fog of human consciousness, understood this both about me and McCullers? And about Mr. Cates, too? I remember him telling us about only one single woman he was going to marry, but they never would have sex.

What did this mean? I must have gone cross-eyed like Miss Amelia. Sex was mentioned in ninth grade public school?

Rumors abounded about all-boys book discussions at his house. Back in the early Sixties, being a homosexual did not exist. Even in the mid-Eighties, when it dawned on me I might prefer women, I had never met a lesbian, at least no one I was aware of. I was afraid I'd have to become a bull dyke and drive a semi.

Finally, after seven months of terror at the desire to kiss a woman's lips, I was overnight in a New York friend's apartment, the next day heading for Europe, when I woke in the middle of the night. I stood up in my friend's living room, looked out at the Hudson River, and asked myself, honestly, Nat, what's going on?

And the immediate answer: I want to try women.

Okay, I said, and the next day I went first thing to a bookstore and purchased a gay guide to Europe.

In each city we visited, my friend Carol—a good sport—and I researched in daylight the address of a hidden lesbian bar that opened at ten or eleven at night. No signs were ever up.

I went back in the dark, by myself, when they opened.

The first was in Madrid, and I only realize now looking back that it must have been an S & M bar. I sidled up to the counter, sat on a stool, ordered a beer—I hated beer—and sipped it slowly, looking around. Burt Lancaster was in chains in a big photo over the cash register. Were these lesbians? It was summer. Everyone seemed to have rolled-up sleeves, hair long and short. I was shy, embarrassed but wanted to stare.

I realize now that big macho Hemingway even had an influence here. I was happy to come to a bar by myself like he did. I'd read about him and wanted to have that freedom and feeling of safety, too. Here I was, finally living it, un-afraid. No danger in this bar, at least. It was all women.

I walked home at midnight, very proud of myself. Next city was Lisbon, where I danced with a cluster of women and someone pulled out a joint. Or was the joint in Bar-celona, where I walked back to the hotel at 3 A.M., seeing a rat run across the boulevard? The last place was Byzan-tium, I think that was the name, in Paris. A twenty-dollar cover charge, which entitled you to one free drink. Wow, those women were gorgeous, and could they dress!

I met one woman from Bangladesh. "Amazing," I said to her. "I didn't know there were lesbians in Bangladesh?"

"That's why I'm here," she laughed.

Eventually I went home with a nineteen-year-old from Canada who always knew she liked girls but was afraid to act on it. I was almost twenty years older but just as afraid. We went back to her hotel, but didn't touch, laid on her bed fully clothed, next to each other.

In the morning, early, I popped up from bed and left. The street sweepers were out, and I purchased a still-hot baguette. Walking back to Carol and my hotel, breaking off the heel of the bread, I thought triumphantly, *I did something.*

Or could it have simply been that Carson McCullers was the only woman we read in all of high school and even most of college, where I majored in English Literature and read mostly white, dead men from England? McCullers gave me a vision that women could write. I had doubted it.

A bench is at the top of the hill I'm climbing. I sit down and look out at a valley below, two roads converging and then lots of trees tangled together. A mountain range in the distance. I lean back and recall in Wisconsin a woman sidling up to me at that Saturday lunch at the end of the writing retreat week.

"Where are you from?" I asked, turning my head, half a sandwich in my hand.

"Illinois."

I remember the joy for me in that workshop was that because it was in Wisconsin, many Midwesterners, who would normally not travel to either coast for a workshop, made it to the center of the country.

"Chicago?"

"Oh, no, a small town south of there."

I nodded, popped a corn chip into my mouth.

"My girlfriend died," she confessed.

"Really? I'm sorry. As in friend or partner?"

"Oh, no." She put her left hand to her mouth. "We were friends. We owned a house together."

Now she had my curiosity.

"So you had separate bedrooms."

"No, we slept together."

I nodded again. This time I stopped eating and gave her my full attention.

"She was very meticulous, and I knew she left full in-structions on how to take care of the house. I know she read your first book. I found her notebooks."

"Oh, so the instructions were in there?"

"Oh, I would never read her notebooks."

"Of course not," I agreed.

"But after six months I did." *Ahh,* now we were getting someplace. I raised my right eyebrow. She continued, "She kept writing to someone named Natalie, asking for help and she told all kinds of things to her."

"Really?" Not for a moment did she mention that 'Natalie' in the notebooks and me, sitting in front of her, was the same person.

"Finally, I thought to look on her computer. Sure enough, there was everything I needed to know about the house."

"So are you trying to date now? Men or women?" I asked.

She seemed a little taken aback. "Oh, I can't date women. You know how society is."

"Fuck society." I decided to go all out for her. "Do what you want. Maybe not where you live, but everyone is coming out one way or another these days."

A small smile crept across her lips.

"I had to come here to meet you. I think you meant so much to my girlfriend. It wasn't easy. How would I get here?"

"How did you get here?"

"Well, I thought, Natalie has come to the Midwest. My co-workers really supported me. I not only had to drive, I had to take a ferry."

"Yeah, that ferry is tricky. Driving a car onto it. You don't travel much?"

She nodded.

"I feel honored that you came." Hand on heart, I meant it.

PART VI

DREAM

EARLY IN AUGUST, a dream:

My father is helping me dig my own grave. We have to be careful to go deep but not wide, because on each side of us is another grave of someone already buried. The whole plot is full of close graves.

My mother joins us and digs. I have tremendous energy for the task and am working hard.

We are done and I immediately say to my mother, "We have to get a casket. I don't want to be buried in only a sheath." I climb out and say to my quarrelsome, much younger brother and sister that they should behave themselves. I'll be gone by tonight and then they can fight and do whatever they want.

It is so clear, vivid, direct, but what does it mean? Am I burying myself? I tell friends my dream. They are haunted, think it's weird, scary. I go to a therapist; we can't figure it out. We make poking attempts that go nowhere. Both my parents have been dead for decades, but in the dream, they are dressed and alive, mostly digging. I don't remember them so wholeheartedly helping me before.

The dream becomes a pebble I have in my mouth, indigestible, that rolls around over my teeth, pushed by my tongue. I let it live back there and hope some resolution will come.

A month later, a cancer scare. My calcium numbers are way high on the quarterly blood test. I stop taking all supplements and a week later retake the test. I'm quite equanimous till the seventh day when they extract blood again. Terror runs through my body, even when I learn I'm okay and Dulcinea, my kind oncologist, calls and emails. The panic rips through my muscles, stomach, liver. I can't stop it. The shaking terror will stop on its own, I know. I have no control.

I thought I had a handle on death—look at my dream. I'm digging my own grave. I know the end will come someday, but now I begin to grieve tree shadows, even opening a bottle of ginger ale, bending to clip toenails, the phone ringing, the damn raccoons with their black face masks sneaking at night into the back garden, picking out the worms with their agile paws through the wire of the compost fence. A tasty protein treat for them. I know I will miss everything someday. It will all be gone. Even the god of song. I won't pick up a pen, word, paper, all gone. Yes, I think I know this, but when the calcium unbalanced, a

117

whole new dance ran through me. This is my body and it simply won't be. Take that, Nat Goldberg. I'm shivering, I don't know anything.

It seemed a long time ago that Eddie and I shared what we will miss when we die. I will miss every single grain of sand. Every cloud. Every person I have known and not known. No one left out.

The dream comes back to me again days later while I'm on a long hike way south of town. I start right out my front door, down to a miserable little stream, sometimes a trickle. We call it the Santa Fe River, but any water, even just the water sound, is good in this environment. I walk along it to the green shuttered house, then across the road and into the wilderness. I'm aiming to climb the back side of a mountain I can see from my bedroom window. The front side of the mountain is where you can properly park your car and hike the Dorothy Stewart Trail, named for the woman who was a member of the Work Projects Administration Artist Collective in New Mexico during the Great Depression. It's the only trail in this area with a woman's name, but five years ago someone smashed the driver's window of my car and stole my purse hidden under the front seat. They left all the groceries in the back of the car. They stole no lettuce, beans, or butter. I never parked there again. I repaired the window and could have parked my car there empty and unlocked, but the main approach to Stewart's trail did not feel right, safe, or comfortable anymore.

I get to the top and look around for a tree I can lean against to meditate. My body no longer can go cross-legged and sit erect on its own steam. A tree helps. I find a craggy stump above the trail, take off my small pack that holds only a water bottle, and settle into my breath. I don't pay much attention to the grand vista of pale blue mountains in the distance. But inside everything is getting very big. I swear I can feel the Earth turn, the moon—I stop. Does the moon circle the sun? I can't remember. Then the sun goes around the Earth? It's all scrambled.

Science, high school, please come back to me. You can hike for miles and see no one here. Naturally I do not have an iPhone with me, and even if I brought one it would never occur to me to look anything up. Yes, maybe I'm arrogant—what if I fell? I'll take my chances. What did we do before the internet? My old Zen teacher:

Modern life is artificially protected. When the artificial environment collapses, for instance in a natural disaster or an economic calamity, people suffer severely. Modern people, therefore, need to live in direct contact with nature and find a practice method in tune with nature's rhythm. Old ways of life fit this purpose. Such a life will put the modern life in a different perspective and teach us how we should live.

I see two hikers below on the trail: "Excuse me." I call out. They look around. "I'm up here." I wave.

They swivel their heads. It's a man and woman, not necessarily a couple. "For a moment I got mixed up. Does the moon go around the sun? And what about the Earth?" I ask them.

They both look stumped for a moment. They weren't expecting this. Then the woman lights up, like it was a whole new discovery. "No! The moon goes around the Earth." She shows me with her hands. "And the Earth goes around the sun."

All three of us are delighted. "Thank you so much. I got confused."

They take off grinning, continuing their hike. Then the man stops abruptly and looks up at me through the tree branches. "Is anything happening up there we should know about?"

"No, no. But if there is, I'll let you know."

They go on their merry way, and I sink into myself again. After a time of rising and falling thoughts, the dream of digging comes back full bore, like a gray whale rising from the deep, over the horizon.

"You, again." Tears behind my eyelids. I understand the dream perfectly. I want to get out of this life. I can't bear what's happening in this world. Destruction and violence have taken over everything. I want out. My parents, who come from a different generation, have come to help. I'm digging with determination, even willing to face choosing the coffin I will lie in.

Excuse me, ladies and gentlemen, I'm afraid it's about the internet again. I remember, maybe fifteen years ago at a conference, someone asked me what I thought of ebooks. At the time I didn't know what they were, but I sighed: "You know, if all of you could just wait twenty years, I'll be dead and you can do whatever you want."

But here's the trick (not a trick but maybe a fuller new angle): In the dream I have a much younger brother and sister, arguing all the time. That's the world I'm leaving. Those kids with all their devices. I dreamed them. In reality I don't have a much younger brother and sister, but those kids have entered my psyche and they are now my blood kin. When I tell them in the dream to please wait, stop fighting, I'll be gone by tonight, they are jolted silent.

I feel the whole dream in moments on that mountainside. The next iteration of humanity. Not good or bad. Memory will be held not by human beings but in machines; you won't know even your close friends', lovers', family's phone numbers. The machine will carry them.

Then what will the human mind be used for? Don't let the commercial world so quickly fill that mind space. Of course, thoughts don't stop. The mind's nature is to create thoughts. But what else? Where are we going? I guess I'm still in it for a while with the bad water in Jackson, Mississippi, Ukraine's terrible war, the floods in Kentucky and Pakistan. Great Britain with no air conditioners and a heat that is uncontrollable. In the dream I do not finally climb into the grave that I've dug and bury myself, nor do I ask my parents or siblings for assistance to go under.

I climb down from the mountain and I walk the long walk home; some of it I lope. A new freedom is in me. I don't have to fight anything anymore. It's all part of me.

PART VII

THE LAKE

something that given to us once, no matter what,
never can be taken back.
—from "Harbor," a poem by Tony Hoagland

On Sunday of Labor Day weekend, Yu-kwan and I drove out to Abiquiu to hike at Ghost Ranch. We'd check out Abiquiu Lake on the way, but I thought that I might not be able to bear looking at it. They had emptied the lake, a reservoir, two years ago. It had broken my heart. The desolation was too painful: the algae, the mud, the dead branches sticking up from the dead trees where there had been a lake in the desert, surrounded by the Pedernal, her long arms extending, holding us. O'Keeffe's ashes were scattered on top and on the land around Ghost Ranch. (Funny how the painter claimed a section of country as hers even when she was long dead.)

So on this holiday weekend, I was stunned to see the

123

lake full and fully functioning with more than the usual visitors.

Before they emptied the reservoir two years ago, I drove out alone three times a week all summer for five years—since my cancer diagnosis. Often, I was the only one there around noon on weekdays. One July I didn't have to wear a bathing suit for the whole month. It was an hour drive each way up north through Española, turning at 84, heading west through Hernandez, where Ansel Adams many years ago caught the famous photograph *Moonrise, Hernandez,* just as the full moon was rising east over the Sangre de Cristos.

Years before they drained Abiquiu, they drained Heron Lake, my first New Mexico summer love, a honey of a place, full of sailboats, no motorboats allowed. It was a longer haul, two hours away, but worth it. But draining Abiquiu was the final straw in my deteriorating relationship with New Mexico—now no water anyplace. The state was like a lover that had betrayed me and denied what I wanted and needed.

Since my mother died, I needed to be near water. Before her death, New Mexico always had an oceanic feeling.

Now I disliked the state with the intensity I had loved it since I first saw its skies and clouds and mountains in 1970. Other breaches of faith had mounted: the perfect Taos Book Shop with creaking wood floors was turned into another art gallery. The café across from the bookshop, Caffé Tazza, forming a lovely patio between the two, closed. The Taos Library, where I wrote *Banana Rose,* abruptly became an art museum, a fine one, but nothing was staying the same. Too many double-wides and prefab houses had been trucked out and dropped on the mesa west of town; a darling little health market became a supermarket.

On old Las Vegas Highway in Santa Fe, a restaurant shuttered, its rent too high, one that had been around forever, the place with the big hamburger slathered with green chile and a long counter with a big window looking out on nothing but pigweed. Once I saw a huge bull snake out that window. Abiquiu Lake's draining undid it for me. My undying devotion to New Mexico was over.

I was done with bone-dry land, but I couldn't quite all-the-way leave. I was in shock. It was as if I were breaking up with a long great love. The thought of selling my house, moving all that I'd accumulated, boggled my mind. In the two years coinciding with Covid, house selling drifted in and out of my intentions. I'd toss out a few notebooks, three torn dish towels, and think I made progress. Before Covid brought everything to a dead stop, I hadn't noticed how restless I was. I was too busy teaching. Now the restlessness in my body was painful to feel, my tremendous impatience, my need to keep moving. *Thrum thrum thrum.* Engine charged with no destination. Where did I think I was going? One Zen teacher thought that restlessness was regret—can't bear what, who, how, where we missed and can't go back.

Hell, I'm full of regret, but really? I did what I did. I lived what I lived. Sure, for writing purposes regret is a tasty provocation—I could fill pages. But regret only rang half true. My old Japanese Zen teacher many years ago said, "Ah, restlessness, the energy of creativity."

But in those last two months back from Port Townsend, home in New Mexico, I reconciled with no water—and probably unconsciously with impermanence. I had my bathtub and that was it. I didn't go searching for chlorinated pools. If water couldn't be out in the wild, I'd forget about it. I stayed close to home, rarely used the car, ate only farmer's market produce. No urge to wander off onto mesas and down arroyos where I'd gone again and again over the years, never getting enough.

As I walked down the road to drop off something at Upaya Zen Center—they were closed tight because of Covid—I noticed that I hadn't been restless for quite a while. What happened to me? I gave up. I surrendered. That's exactly what I did. I took pleasure in the last squeeze of toothpaste running out of the tube; the soap someone gave me from Estonia, growing smaller with each hand-washing; every leaf of lettuce I used up, none rotting in the bottom bin; the long walks in the neighborhood; putting away dishes.

I yielded to no place to get wet, no sprinkler to run through. This was a dry place. I let go. I came to peace in the place I loved. Summer would not be like my childhood when five days out of seven we drove south, then west on interstates to Jones Beach, like everyone else on Long Island, packing in on a small section of sand with our blankets and chicken sandwiches wrapped in waxed paper. Never a lawn chair. We either rode the dark ocean waves or sat hunched on our checked picnic blanket in our one-piece bathing suits.

But there was a secret to my newfound peace: I was writing again after almost two dead years. Writing was coming back. I never knew before to be grateful. One book after another. I see now I fed off the energy of my workshops—they gave my writing direction. But something happened lately, a shift inside me, and I felt the lord of song, of inspiration actually breathe in me again. I'd heard all this talk about being filled with breath, being inspired, that the breath was breathing you. Yeah, yeah. I put my money on practice. Keep practicing. But in those two years of intense Covid, practice evaded me. Now all at once I was writing again, filled with happiness. I kept whispering *thank you, thank you,* and I did feel full of breath, breathing me.

The writing was what allowed me to look again like a solid citizen of daily life. The dipping deep down inside was what sustained me, gave me serenity.

And then that Sunday we stopped by Abiquiu Lake on Labor Day weekend, planning to hike at Ghost Ranch, and like a mirage the lake was full again. I ripped off my clothes and dived in in my underwear. It was more wonderful, more beautiful than I even remembered. Layers of salmon and pink cliffs in the distance and hardly any ripples. Calm, open. I'd had something I loved so deeply and fully, and it was taken away. Not for a moment, like dropping an ice cream cone, but for two whole years. And I had even let go (I do not let go so easily)—and here it was—the lake—back. I felt like a jigsaw puzzle, whole but broken. I could not comprehend. The lake here? Back? I was like a dragon sensing the water. I dropped everything. Forget serenity. I'd come every day. Smash any appointments. Nothing else mattered. Let the corn and zucchinis rot in the vegetable bin in the fridge. I got back what I never imagined getting back.

I had to make the most of it before the cold settled in. I had at least three weeks. For the whole last week I drove the hour blasting Dylan's *Oh Mercy* "Ring Them Bells." All day by myself. I wanted to meet the lake alone, to make sense of coming and going, of having it again.

Then I called a new Zen teacher in town. "You have to see this. When are you free all day?" We would go that Thursday, right after I had a double booster for my immune system in a back room of the hospital in case the vaccine I had gotten two weeks before didn't work. I had to wait an hour to make sure there were no reactions to the booster. I snuck out after forty-five minutes. "I'm going to the lake," I called back to the nurse. My friend didn't have a bathing suit—she just moved here from Texas. Of course she didn't have a bathing suit. As a foregone conclusion, I figured that the state next to mine had no fun. Everyone was busy prohibiting abortions and closing down open learning of history in the public schools.

We jumped in my car. I packed it with two folding chairs, noodles—foam strips for floating—sunscreen (she was fair skinned), water bottles, a banana, apples from the backyard tree, and river shoes to walk on the rocks.

I told her, "I am going to try to not say a lot about where we are going, so you can be surprised and let it all unfold in front of you." After driving for forty minutes, the top of the Pedernal peeked like a great oculus over a mesa in front of it. I pointed it out. "Guess whose ashes are up there."

She couldn't imagine.

I said O'Keeffe's name and she turned in her seat in awe. "New Mexico." I nodded. "Someone awake was looking at this land."

I warned her, "We come to a very steep downhill, but don't worry, right at the bottom is a quick left." We parked and gathered all our equipment together from the car trunk. Weighed down, we headed for the swimming area. Over the hump and then the shift to soft ground. As we got closer it was evident something had changed, but I couldn't comprehend it. I had left the lake the night before at six thirty, almost evening. But before us was a drained lake, algae already forming on the periphery.

"It's gone," a woman in a drooping tent on a rock exposure said.

I recognized her. The day before she had been in a

kayak, told me she had leave from the military, originally from Puerto Rico.

I stared. This couldn't be true. It was true. It was man-made and they took it away. Overnight. I lost it again. I got a taste of the cool deep water—then it was gone. My Zen friend was standing next to me.

I knew what to do. "Do you want to sit?" I asked.

We returned our stuff to the car and climbed up to the pavilion. A cement floor and a tin roof and two long wooden picnic tables with attached long benches. Another table perpendicular to the other two and a stone chimney where you can barbecue. A weekday. No one around, especially now that the lake was gone.

Big vista from up there. We didn't look much. We bowed, sat at two ends of one bench, and went below discursive thought like going under water, our eyes unfocused. We sat still. What else could we do? I hoped my body could find repair from the jerk of discovery then disappearance of the lake within days—my life had been gladly scrambled for the lake's presence.

The slightest pitter-patter on the metal roof; the smallest shower from a single cloud above our heads. Then silence. Then another shower, like someone tossing a handful of pebbles on the roof. But quieter than pebbles. If we weren't still, we might never have heard it.

Then, after a half hour of sitting, we slow-walked around the picnic tables, lifting a foot and placing it down. The other foot. How lucky we were to have two feet. Ten minutes we circled the square tables, slow as clouds with no wind. Then we sat again. Settled in, said nothing.

I could feel the air, the land, the state I loved. The very slight breeze on my arms. The sun and heat were just beyond the shadow cast by the tin roof we sat under. But the shadow was always cool in a dry land. Time opened. The lake was a good thing and now there was no lake. There was this and not this. The great stillness of New Mexico. The absolute real magic, real draw under everything else was how still, how motionless, unmoving, becalmed this land could be. And it showed off for us, matched our immobile sitting moment for moment. We did not sit alone. We sat with everything, including the mirage of a lake and the mirage of our lives. *Tick tick ticking* away.

That night I emailed Eddie the whole story. He is away in France. Eddie writes, "I can't believe it. How can they just drain a lake, like a bathtub? Natalie, I'm so sorry. I really understand how much it meant to you."

What can I say: my summer in this wide-open space of New Mexico, like the mind of god, empty.

PART VIII

READING IT WRONG

I COULDN'T DO it right away—I was too raw—but two months later I drove out past the lake entrance and walked into the Abiquiu dam office.

"What's happening?" I asked the young woman, the only person in the front room. She was sitting behind a big computer. My vision of her face moved in and out as she bent forward or punched the keys. At one point she called someone in the back room to clarify an agreement.

"The water gets purchased from either Albuquerque or Texas. We can't keep the native water. They call and we release it through the Rio Grande down to where it is needed. They can drain as much as they want."

"Why Texas?" I ask.

"Texas had an earlier agreement for water, even before Albuquerque. There's also the San Juan/Chama Divergent Act. The dam was built in 1963." She gave me a number to call if I wanted to check water levels before I came.

I walked out into the bright late-October sun. The water

level had a logical determination. It was contingent on a big city and the adjacent state. You mean water was purchased in orderly amounts? I'd been filled with a wild love. Nature was all I had, and it was disappearing. Warmer temperatures, less snowpack, and limited precipitation had all reduced Rio Grande water levels in recent years.

The Navajos were relocated to the Bosque Redondo a long time ago. The San Juan River bordered much of their northern reservation. They, too, had a claim. The more I read, the more complicated it was. The San Juan begins in Colorado. No place was exempt. The West was in trouble. Too many people; too little water. Texas claimed that New Mexico farmers were illegally pumping underground water that should end up in the Rio Grande, headed for El Paso and West Texas. There were all kinds of judicial hearings and contracts. I knew that water was a problem. Why didn't I consider any of this years ago when the lake had been drained?

Don't expect fairness, I told myself. Was it in public school that we learned the idea of fairness? The other thing I now tell myself: don't expect logic. It's a good idea, but human behavior doesn't seem to run on logic or fairness. Maybe that's how I changed in the last two years? One plus one doesn't equal two—it equals a squirrel.

I did return to Port Townsend (my returns were now all on my dime, no more residencies through Centrum in Fort Worden), and the first time I wrote only in the Reveille Café, the only one in the area to open after Covid closed everything. Very few people came to the two square tables and four wooden chairs. I ordered a tall chamomile tea every morning for $2.49 and put a dollar in the tip jar for the young woman behind the counter. When I barely slept at all the night before I also ordered a coffee, plain, and sipped it. It didn't help wake me up, but it gave some hope at the possibility.

The next two times, in addition to that single café, I added the Carnegie Library in Uptown. The rich man from back east had a long philanthropic reach, and I appreciated it. From the second floor at a wide table, I could look out and see the bay, the sailboats on good days, and always the white and green Whidbey Ferry chugging back and forth. At the library before I wrote for the day, I'd read *The New Yorker* for free. If there was a good cat cartoon, I'd hustle down to the first floor and copy it for ten cents at the copy machine and send it to my friend back home.

Once when I walked the two blocks there from where I was staying, I saw a bumper sticker on an old VW van: *We are not all here, because we are not all there.* I thought about that for a long time, trying to imagine where they could be. Oregon? Idaho? One early evening walking home it dawned on me: I missed the whole gist. They were talking about their minds, not a place, *we are not all there.* Then I found out I read it wrong to begin with. It was *We are all here, because we are not all there.* It was describing the people in Port Townsend. In the end it *was* about place, and it was also about their minds. Wasn't this true of all places? No matter what, we have to contend with our minds.

PART IX

EPILOGUE

WHAT THE PANDEMIC gave me, besides tremendous fear, was time and space. I had been so busy all my life, especially the last thirty-five years, traveling to teach all over the country and the world—and when I was home, I worked on a book. I loved it all, but then it seemed my mortality was right under my nose. Did anything else matter?

I don't know why I thought in the deep recesses of my mind that I would live forever. I guess on a good day a lot of us feel that way, but I began to notice when I went to a museum and loved someone's work, I quickly calculated how old they were when they died: Helen Frankenthaler, 1928–2011, age 83; Joan Mitchell (not the singer, but the painter), American, lived most of her life in France, 1925–1992, she died at 67, young; Susan Rothenberg, 1945–2020, 75, American painter who lived in Galisteo, New Mexico, near me. I was stunned to see Rothenberg's dates after her name, a jolt to my body as I stood in front of her painting in the Phillips Collection, Washington, D.C. She smoked a lot; Mitchell drank. I tried to rationalize. No matter; I knew at the bottom of every life a limitless moan played out, however we were able to deal with it, face it or not face it—and that it wasn't our place to get arrogant, judgmental, thinking we knew someone else's life.

Can I tell you that I also went to a horse's grave in Lexington, Kentucky? Secretariat's. Usually a great race-horse's heart, head, and hooves are buried, but Secretariat was buried at nineteen, whole, at Claiborne Farm, which is considered a great honor.

Obviously, horses have a very different life span. It was a relief to imagine another being buried there, other than a human.

Secretariat, nicknamed Big Red, won the Triple Crown in 1973 and still holds the fastest record for all three races. Mostly men at Claiborne Farm told me about a race-horse's heart, the capacity of the blood pumping through it as the horse ran. Secretariat's heart was estimated to weigh twenty-two pounds, twice the size of an average horse's. On that visit they kept repeating to me that Secretariat won the Belmont by thirty-one lengths. He was so far ahead in the end that his jockey, Ron Turcotte, actually turned to look behind because suddenly there were no horses around them. So many years later the enthusiasm was still palpable.

My father's racing enthusiasm passed down to his daughter. My father was buried in 1999 in a Hebrew cemetery in the family plot, coincidentally very near to Belmont Park. The shouts at the racetrack could be heard over my father's grave. His daughter no longer believed in the races after understanding how they hurt the thoroughbreds. If my father were still alive, I'm sure he would have responded, "That's malarkey. They were made to race." That was an old way of thinking, but Secretariat was a glory. He's the only animal whose grave I ever went to. (No, never even a dog's or cat's.)

Other species and beings have different life spans. Grass has this one summer; not the same grass comes back. A fly's life span is twenty-eight days; a blue whale—the biggest whale, with a heart almost the size of a small piano—lives many years. Let us not forget the common Brown House Moth, which lives one to six months, or the Ponderosa pine—its bark smelling of vanilla or butterscotch—which can live, if it's lucky, up to five hundred years. Do trees have luck? Do we? Or is it a preponderance of circumstances?

In the days of my retirement, in that space that opened up, I remembered I always had a dream of riding the Canadian train across Canada. It didn't pan out because of the loosening mask protocol. I had to continue to be so careful with chronic, though mostly latent (fingers crossed), cancer. But my friend and I decided to fly to Montreal anyway.

Tired of the necessary use of the internet for navigation,

on the fifth day in that old and venerable city, I went out to wander on my own. In the back of my mind, I was going to find Leonard Cohen's grave. A big picture of him was reflected on a downtown building. You could feel the pride and appreciation of this singer/songwriter in the city's life. I knew he returned often to his birth town. I had a general direction of where the cemetery was and headed out by foot.

Leonard called me in the mid-Eighties in Taos when *Writing Down the Bones* was first published. I was in retreat with my Zen teacher on the bluffs of the Mississippi near Iowa and missed his call. When my second book, *Wild Mind,* came out, I contacted him for a blurb. I was young and never forgot his gracious reply on the telephone: "I have so many talented friends. Don't worry, you are on your way."

In Montreal that day, I wanted to honor him. That has been my practice with many artists, to honor them by searching out their final resting place, whether only their bones—and teeth—after many years might be left, or their ashes gathered in one place.

Cohen's would be a full body burial, no cremation, the only kind allowed in a serious Jewish cemetery.

I took my time. I love to wander and get lost. As I left the busy Rue Saint Laurent behind, I asked two people about "A big cemetery?" Each pointed in opposite directions. I followed a hunch, the old way of direction, at the periphery of a long-standing neighborhood with a bakery café on a corner, stopping for refreshment: a rather large éclair. "Cemetery?" I inquired again as I paid my bill.

A shrug of shoulders, turn of the head, from the woman behind the croissants. "Maybe that way," she pointed over the golden rolls.

I faced a steep hill. I just knew that at the top, behind the established tall brick homes, was what I was looking for. A deep sigh. *C'mon,* I gave myself a little encouragement. After all, this was sea level, much lower and easier for climbing than my home at 7,000 feet.

Early November, not winter cold, still green, but tired grass among so many gravestones; *Cohen* is a recurring surname. I see one after the other in the endless rows. I meet, I surmise, a young college student, the only other person in this fading afternoon. "Are you looking for the same grave as I am?" He nods. "How about you go this way," I point, "and I go that." We both take off.

A bit later, he shyly approaches me. "I think I found it."

He takes me rows down and indicates with a nod of his head where it is, then oddly disappears.

The light is fading. Leonard Cohen is buried next to his mother. There is a big family Cohen stone, but he also has his own, 1934–2016. I calculate: 82 years old. Pretty good, and rare for a star to still be close to his family, but he always stayed connected to his roots. I also know he practiced as a Zen monk for six years in the dry hills outside Los Angeles.

Of all the graves I visited, this had by far the most par-aphernalia that I had ever seen. People left coins, stones, crystals, notes, feathers, marking their visit. Hebrew let-tering, more traditional, was carved in the flat stone next to his mother's, and then on his own separate headstone was his name carved large and HALLELUJAH in caps in yellow at the bottom.

I was happy to be there. I was in Japan when he died; my two friends and I—one Canadian, one Filipino—listened to his songs when he died, our ears against a staticky tap-ing. This felt like a completion.

I looked to my right. A slight woman stood back in the shadows. "Am I taking up the space?" I asked.

"No, no." She came forward. "It's his sixth memorial today, so I brought him flowers." She indicated with a nod. Fresh ones were lying in the dirt.

"Oh, I didn't realize that." I tilted my head.

"Where are you from?" I asked her.

"Do you know Upaya Zen Center? My sister lived there for ten years. Did you know her? Maria—they called her—Rinzan. She returned to Canada, to her family. She died of cancer. I'm from around here."

Now we were out of the darkening cemetery, walking downhill on the sidewalk. "I think I knew your sister. She wore glasses, was a monk, shaved head? I live down the road from Upaya Zen Center.

"She loved Roshi Joan's dog Dominga and stayed with him a full winter up at the Zen land by herself. She adored

Joan Halifax, and our whole family was so thankful that she and Shinzan called in her last days. It was a great blessing and she was so thankful.

"She was a very serious Zen student? A bit judgmental of everyone else? She thought they were wimps because she was so strong physically and never missed a period of Zen?" I was trying to picture her.

I remembered she could do the work of three people in the garden. She learned from my friend Wendy all about winter squash and had a joy of harvesting.

"Every summer she'd come home to Toronto to renew her visa and see family. I know she tenderly took care of Dominga's grave, buried in Upaya's grounds."

We turned a corner. I followed Maria's sister and listened. Her sister's death was still fresh. I think she had died about six months before.

"Let me take you out to lunch tomorrow," she said. "We can go to a deli Leonard frequented and I can show you his place nearby."

I was in a daze, not quite able to digest this coincidence, and I also couldn't fully picture her sister. All of it felt very eerie initiating in a graveyard at dusk. "Sure," I said.

We set it for noon. She gave me directions. "What's your name?" she asked. I told her. "The writer?" I nodded. She let out a scream. "My sister read your books and gave them to me." She put a hand over her mouth in disbelief.

The next day she brought photos.

"Ahh, yes, that's her," I said, recognizing her sister. "I thought so. Yeah, there she is."

"She faced right into death, accepted it, very fierce."

She clearly had a need to talk about her sister's death to someone who knew her in New Mexico, and I wanted to hear about her death, to help alleviate the suffering. I was someone who lived down the road for ten years. It was an honor.

She then told me about first meeting Leonard, way before he was so popular. They were both young. She'd heard some of his songs and was stunned by them. Somehow, her work at the time—I couldn't understand what it was—allowed her to find out what time he was flying in to Montreal. She brought a huge bouquet—she showed me with her arms how big—to the airport and saw him with two friends across baggage claim. She said her knees were knocking loud, she was trembling so much. Leonard saw all the flowers and said to his friends, "Wow, can you imagine who is so lucky?" He really had no idea.

She presented the flowers to Leonard Cohen and they were friends ever since.

PART X

ADDENDUM

TWO YEARS AFTER Eddie and I met at the Water History Park nearby, we were sitting in my living room. I still hadn't been to my friend Helen's group residence. She had just turned ninety. Eddie told me, "You better apply. Your memory wasn't so good back at the Park."

I sighed, not as interested in travel, enjoying staying put in New Mexico. "C'mon, Eddie, let's ask each other five words again." Though the plan of moving to California seemed like a long shot now. Covid was almost over, and I could move around more in the land I loved.

He shook his head *no,* but I was already walking across the room to get a paper and pencil.

He slowly wrote five words down, looking around, hoping to spy in my house disconnected objects so I couldn't remember them by association. He then doggedly repeated them to me twice. I listened carefully, nodding my head after each one. "Okay, let's talk for a while," he said. We needed conversation in between to test memory.

I sat on my hands. He told me about a trip he and Mary were taking. I asked questions, all the while in the back of my head clinging to the words.

"Okay, what are they?" he asked.

I spit out, "*Jungle, liquid.* What's the middle one? I know. I know. *Horse!*" A pause. "*Glove.* Huh, the last one? *Bread!*" I yelled. I was so pleased you'd have thought I had won the Kentucky Derby.

I gave Eddie his words and, like before, he was able to recall them. Of course, he had nothing at stake. His plan was not to move into a retirement home.

"Do you want to hear mine again?" I asked as he was about to leave. I shot ahead: "*Jungle, liquid, horse, glove, bread,*" I listed, like a real champion. I paused. "I can feel my mind is more toned."

"Yeah, I can feel your brain is different. What did you do?"

I shook my head. "I don't know."

Later that night I realized it was reading. In the last months I had read a lot of good, sometimes difficult, sometimes thick, books. Earnestly, patiently, determined. Books I wanted to read but never got around to. Books I wanted to read before I died. *Black Boy* by Richard Wright, *A Tale of Love and Darkness* by Amos Oz, *Dalva* by Jim Harrison, *The Master* by Colm Tóibín, *The Portrait of a Lady* by Henry James, *Jane Eyre* by Charlotte Brontë, *Apeirogon* by Colum McCann, *Lab Girl* by Hope Jahren, *Blood, Bones & Butter* by Gabrielle Hamilton,

The Bluest Eye by Toni Morrison, *The Parisian* by Isabella Hammad.

I began to feel tremendous empathy for the writers, how hard it was to finish writing a book, to make writing your life's work. I'd turn front face in a bookstore any book I had just read. I became a writer's best friend. I remember after *Dalva,* thinking, *Jim can't do it for himself anymore.* Jim Harrison died in 2016, age 78, literally as he was writing. He had a writing utensil clutched in his hand and fell over from a heart attack, the ink mark trailing across the page.

I remembered something I read in *The New York Times* decades ago and often repeated to my students: *"Reading is the highest activity of the mind."*

I felt it physically, how much more toned my mind felt, and even Eddie could feel it.

When I paid attention, words had gravitational weight; they were not flighty and forgotten but like jewels, rooted, held in the crown of my head.

A *WRITING ON EMPTY* ROAD MAP:
WRITING INSTRUCTIONS

WRITING ON EMPTY is my migration out of not being able to write. I try not to call it "writer's block" because that is too much of a solidification, and that term has a long history connected with fear. Best to stay light, try not to freeze the hand—and mind—in bewildering times. Best to let *writing do writing* and get out of the way.

This Road Map is based on my process, and it aims to point you back to your writing sources, the places in your life that can inspire you to remember and create.

I have taught in-person, human-to-human for fifty years. What has struck me over and over with hundreds of people is how desperate they are to complete their story, to believe they are someone, that they matter. I see this anxiety everywhere, around the world, in every group of students.

First, I want to say before we go any further, before

anything, that you matter. You are alive. You have breath. If you believe this, we can go on.

This Road Map presents a writing practice that builds a writing spine. Once you have that, you can direct your writing wherever you want. I have explained this in person and to all the many people on little squares on Zoom when I have taught online, even before Covid. Recently, I was asked to visit the online course again for four consecutive Sundays from eleven to noon Mountain Time.

In the fourth—and last—encounter with this online Sunday group, I asked them to list any details they remembered from a portion of an essay I read to them by Chang-Rae Lee, recalling his mother's cooking after she died.

I chose a student with a long name to read his list. But first I asked, "Where are you?"

"Bulgaria."

"Bul-gar-ia." I don't think I had ever pronounced that name and it felt delightful in my mouth. I wasn't sure where it was but how I loved the word. I repeated it, "Bul-ga-ria."

He read his list. He was a bit shy but happy. Then quickly, "I have a question." I had told them, "Just read your list," lickety-split, no comments.

"But how can I deny someone from Bulgaria?" I got to pronounce it again.

But then I shook my head *no* and we went on to a young

woman from Queens, then India. I felt these people, even through this machine, this zoom zam thank you ma'am internet. I felt their need and longing for more guidance, directions into publication. "You know I teach writing *practice*," I told them over and over.

So, let's use this very *book* in your hands (or in your ear) to see how the form was built through writing practice. Of course, you must continue to show up, keep the hand moving—and it's good to use writing topics.

PART I: THE WRITER'S PANDEMIC

You can see Natalie realized the value in the *structure* of meeting her friend Eddie repeatedly at the nearby park during the pandemic. When Eddie was injured in his bike accident, the structure broke open. She missed seeing him in person. They had established a rootedness together. When the structure of their meetings broke, it broke open the way she was seeing her life, the past, the present. There was space for her to realize compassion for her mother, something she never felt before.

Now you: Write about a moment when you understood something about a member of your family or even yourself—how hard your grandfather's immigration was or the misery you went through moving to a new school when you were young, why your aunt was crazy or how

fundamentally you always loved your uncle Sam. Keep going; don't break and get scared.

What structure do you do repeatedly that you can rely
on during hard times? Brush your teeth? Drink coffee?
Tie the laces of your shoes? Write about that and keep
your hand moving. Stay specific and go where your mind
takes you. Discover the answer, rather than having the answer ahead of time.

PART II: THE CEMETERY

What writers had an elemental influence on your life?
Who, even years after you read them, you remember their
impact. Talk to one of them in writing, tell them how important they were to you. What else do you want to say?
Go ahead, pour out your heart to them. What was your
life like when you read their work?

Give background: *I was in my second year of college,
miserable, majoring in engineering . . .* or, *It was autumn.
I sat by the thundering Niagara, your book on my lap, page
121 . . .* or begin, *I never wanted to read you . . .*

The author can be dead or alive. For Natalie, Idaho
was that mysterious place where all literature coalesced,
but she'd never been there before she went to Hemingway's grave.

Tell about a place you've never been, one you never
imagined going to . . .

PART III: CENTRUM RESIDENCY

Natalie mentions a tender memory she had about her partner. Write about a first kiss, a last kiss, someone's shoulder revealed, a knee, the space around your heart.

What author have you recently read more than one of their books? If you want to write, you have to read—essays, poems, novels, whatever is out there. Remember: *Authors are our teachers.* How did they build whatever you are reading? Notice this.

Find one writer you love and study their writing. What attracts you? Is it familiar from your own mind—even more, from your own life? Are you a city person who longs to live in mountains or vice versa? Books can take you where you might not be able to afford to go. Africa. China. The Philippines. Into the horrors of war. The orchards of California.

Writing and reading is all mind-to-mind transmission. No limits. Drop your ideas—and yourself—and submerge yourself into the deep pleasure of entering the writer's mind when you read.

In *Writing on Empty* Part III, Natalie delights in spending a whole month on her own. It's not always easy to be in solitude. Can you give yourself a half day? Put it on your calendar and keep that date with yourself.

Don't run from loneliness. Being alone is the writer's *métier*; even at a party, some part of us is studying, watching, listening—make good use of it later, pen to paper, fingers to keyboard. What has been your experience of loneliness, of being alone? Write about it.

In *Writing on Empty,* Natalie talks about her trepidation about the internet and her coming to some kind of peace with it. How has the internet affected you? Write about it. Negatively, positively, or you don't know because you were born into it. What would it be like to not have it?

Dirt by Bill Buford brought Natalie into the heart of French cooking. Write about a foreign country you traveled to or experienced through a book or movie that filled your imagination.

Write about your favorite foods. Write about what you know how to cook, even if it's Jell-O from the box—or macaroni and cheese, from a box.

At the end of Part III, Natalie goaded her friend Eddie to talk about what he will miss when he dies. They kept their connection, though Eddie had been changed by his accident. How have you kept connections with friends? What will you miss when you die? Go for at least ten minutes or longer. Be detailed.

PART IV: ELK

Driving home from Port Townsend, Natalie and her partner stopped in a rainforest in the Olympic National Forest and encountered Roosevelt elk, close up. She had a deep identity connection with one of the magnificent females.

What animals do you feel close to? What animals live with you? Write about this. Be specific.

Natalie also visited the Portland Art Museum and took her time with the images of Mount St. Helens and the Japanese pottery.

What is it you spend slow time examining? And if you don't, why not?

She mentions time connected to the ceramic pots, but also in reference to her mother's age.

How old are you? Feel it, whatever age. And your birthday, what is your attitude? Many people have angst around their birthdays. Write fully what you feel about your birthday.

And what simply is your relationship to time? Do you fight it, run from it, wrestle with it or try to control time? Talk about that in your writing.

Like her friend Grove, have you felt lost? When? At every age you can step into the void, feeling helpless, out of control. What's been your experience?

She writes about sitting with her mother in a deli. Tell about an experience you had in a café, restaurant, coffee shop. Don't forget to mention what was hanging on the wall. You are not sure? Make it up. Check it later. Just keep writing. (Of course, you can't make everything up unless it's fiction, but what's a good guess?)

PART V: QUEER

How has the world changed for you—and around you—since the pandemic?

Where do you go walking? Even if it's just crossing streets, write about it. Strong memories came up for Natalie as she walked.

What strong memories—good and bad—come up for you? Write about them, share them, give the details. You might begin with "I remember" and follow what comes up. Let the mind unfold your memories. Every time you get stuck, come back to "I remember" and keep going.

Natalie's thoughts, especially in *Writing on Empty,* are connected to books and authors. In a way it's how she climbed out of the pandemic dilemma and the suffering all around her.

Write about how you climb out of suffering. What tools do you use? Name your great friends, not always people. Mountains, a comfortable chair, a kite can also be a friend.

Natalie realizes as she walks and remembers that the author Carson McCullers had more of an effect on her when she read her book in ninth grade than she knew. What connections have surprised you? Write about this. What are you very ignorant about? Are you willing to admit it? What are you embarrassed by? Can you write it down even if you never show anyone?

Is there something about your internal life that you're only realizing years later? Maybe you were not aware of it for a long time, the way Natalie only realized about herself and Carson and Mr. Cates many years later. Sometimes writing is the method for unfolding your past; it's actually ahead of you.

Natalie uses going to Europe as a way to break free and accept her desires. Where do you break free? What is breaking free for you? Of course, write about it.

Has anyone told you a secret? Do you have secrets? You can write about this and never show anyone.

What do you do when you fly? Natalie often reads books. But maybe you don't fly—especially since Covid, it seems more difficult. So what do you do when waiting in a doctor's office, or an unemployment office, or on a long drive when you are not the driver? Write.

PART VI: DREAM

What current night dreams have been haunting your daylight hours? Or is there some very old dream that persists in your consciousness, one you can't make sense of, like a loose tooth you keep nudging with your tongue?

Write about it. Write about it from different angles, from different characters and objects in the dream, from their viewpoints, even a wall in a house, or a tree outside, if they are in your dream.

What about your daydreams? What are they? Write.

How do you feel about the climate catastrophe? Write about that, see where it takes you. How is weather different where you live from anywhere else? Why is that?

Let's ask it again: What will you miss when you die? Natalie talks about it in a whole different manner in this part. You must realize that you can write about a topic over and over again.

Have you ever gone hiking on your own? Or taken a long walk in the city by yourself? It might be a good or daring thing to do.

PART VII: THE LAKE

What have you loved deeply, depended on—and lost? Write about this.

Tell about a specific time you went swimming, or why you can't swim, or why you love or hate it. What memories do you have of summer? Tell about your bathing suits. Don't have any? Tell about that.

Only in facing our own suffering can we be free to move on, to help others. The world needs our help. What feels like the best way for you to help? Write about that. Stay close. What is real for you?

What does it mean to you to be *empty*? Pen to paper or fingers to keys. Go.

PART VIII: READING IT WRONG

Natalie goes to the dam office that operates her beloved Abiquiu Lake to get a realistic understanding of why it was suddenly empty. She needed facts to ground herself after losing the lake a second time.

Write about a situation where you reacted emotionally, and how as time passed you became clearer, more intelligent, grounded. Maybe a breakup, a divorce, a car wreck?

Natalie writes about her confusion with the message on a bumper sticker—she misread it and contemplated the wrong gist of the slogan.

Write about your own confusion—at any level. What was going on with your parents in your childhood, an email you misunderstood, the wrong directions to cook a special dinner?

Write about how you unwind confusion, misunderstanding. What steps do you take?

PART IX: EPILOGUE

What graves have you been to? This is a touchy topic. Write about graves of people who are close and immediate; graves of those distant and admired; human and animal.

PART X: ADDENDUM

How can reading be the highest activity of the mind? Break it down. What is the process a person undergoes to read words on a page?

Most of all, Natalie wants you writing. She drew this Road Map to help. After you've done these exercises, she says you can forget these questions, enter your own deep life, and keep your hand—or hands (as in typing)—moving.

AND ONE MORE THING:
NOTE TO READERS

I DON'T KNOW about you, but all my life I've been longing to daydream, even when I didn't realize it. I remember
glancing out the big windows (lucky to have them) in ele-
mentary school but being called back immediately to the
multiplication table. Even Katagiri Roshi, my wonderful
Zen teacher straight from a Japanese monastery, admon-
ished doodling, saying, "It's laziness. Get to work."

But so many years later I can say that he was wrong.
It's so much bigger than laziness—and also, what's so bad
about a bit of a lazy streak? It's a time to digest through
the body our fast-moving world.

After running to the farmer's market at 7 A.M. this
morning, then answering the phone and the doorbell ringing at the exact same second, I finally settled down into a
chair for a moment with no direction, and I noticed how
my body appreciated it. It's called relaxing. Twenty years
ago, a wise therapist said to me, "When you learn to relax,

we will be finished." I tried so hard these last few years, lying on a couch, slumping in a chair, then dodging up right away, recalling beets burning in the oven, a note I have to write, a condolence call—and always in summer some nip and tuck in the garden, deadheading roses, pulling out sprouting aspen seeds in the wrong place.

So right now, can you do this?

Begin with five minutes a day. Drop yourself, lose control. It has to be in the day; thus, *daydreaming.*

Dream off in the big, sometimes-polluted, sometimes-raining sky. If not outside, then over yonder to the other side of the room.

It is available in all places. Costs nothing. Goes nowhere. Helps us deeply.